Metropolitan Area Networks

Matthew N. O. Sadiku, Ph.D.
Associate Professor
Department of Electrical Engineering
Temple University
Philadelphia, Pennsylvania

CRC Press
Boca Raton   Ann Arbor   London   Tokyo

Library of Congress Cataloging-in-Publication Data

Sadiku, Matthew N. O.
   Metropolitan Area Networks / Matthew N. O. Sadiku
     p. cm.
   Includes bibliographical references and index.
   ISBN 0-8493-2474-2
   1. Metropolitan area networks (Computer networks). I. Title.
TK5105.85.S24 1994
004.6'7—dc20
DNLM/DLC
for Library of Congress   94-34033
                                                CIP

No claim to original U.S. Government works
International Standard Book Number 0-8493-2474-2
Library of Congress Card Number 94-34033
Printed in the United States of America 1 2 3 4 5 6 7 8 9 0
Printed on acid-free paper

Dedicated to

Professor Charles K. Alexander
whose mentorship and friendship have greatly enriched my career.

Preface

The last few years have witnessed a growing demand for communication networks. The population of network users has expanded from scientists and engineers to include administrators and secretaries using word processors. Local area networks (LANs) and wide area networks (WANs) are well-established communication networks to meet the increasing demand for communication. Local area networks provide communication services to stations within a limited geographical area and operate at high data rates with simple protocols. Wide area networks provide long-haul communication services across a nation or around the globe and operate at much lower speeds with relatively complex protocols.

There is a need for an intermediate network that operates over a metropolitan area at comparatively high data rates and with reasonable protocol complexity. With some characteristics of LANs and some of WANs, the metropolitan area network (MAN) technology embraces the best features of both. MANs are public networks that are targeted to provide high-speed networking over metropolitan area distances. The MAN effort was started in 1982, about two years after IEEE Project 802 was initiated. The functional goals were to provide for interconnection of LANs, bulk data transfer, digitized voice, and video as well as conventional terminal traffic.

Currently, information on MANs is scattered in standards documents, technical journals, and conference proceedings. A single source of reference for a broad understanding of metropolitan area networks is hard to come by, perhaps because no one seems to know where MAN technology is heading. Although MANs are still evolving in topology, data rates, and above all access protocols, enough is known to warrant documentation.

The major objective of the book is to provide an introduction to the key concepts of metropolitan area networks in a manner that is easily digestible for a beginner in the field. The book should also serve as a single source of reference to the veteran in the area. It is hoped that the book will be beneficial to practicing engineers, computer scientists, and information business managers. The book may also be used for a one-semester graduate course on metropolitan area networks. If used as a textbook for a course, the main prerequisite for students is an introductory course on local area networks (LANs).

The book has five chapters. Chapter 1 provides introductory and background information about MANs. Chapter 2 is devoted to interworking devices, MAN topologies, and key issues facing MAN technology. Some of the popular protocols proposed for MANs are discussed in

Chapter 3. Chapter 4 presents the modeling and performance analysis of common MAN topologies. The last chapter covers emerging MAN-related technologies such as BISDN, ATM networks, frame relay, cell relay, SONET, and SMDS.

Acknowledgments

It is always a difficult task to write about a fast-changing technology. This book is not an exception. I have been greatly assisted by the comments of friends and reviewers who read various parts of the manuscript at different stages. Although every effort has been made to incorporate the most important and recent developments, any omissions are entirely mine.

I want to thank Dr. Zheng Liu, Dr. Oliver Ibe, Dr. Vincent Bemmel, Raymond Jongakiem, Shahrukh Murad, and A. S. Arvind for their comments and suggestions which helped to improve the clarity of the work. I would like to express my gratitude to Professor S. O. Ajose, head of Department of Electrical and Computer Engineering at Federal University of Technology, Minna, Nigeria, where I spent one year, for his support while working on this project. Special thanks go to Dr. Clarence Obiozor and Dr. Saroj Biswas for helping me obtain relevant literature from the United States while I was on leave in Nigeria. I acknowledge the patience and understanding of Bob Stern of CRC Press who brought this book into production; it has been a pleasure working with Bob. Finally, I would like to thank my wife, Chris, and my daughters, Ann and Joyce, for their support.

Table of Contents

Chapter 1

Introduction

Nothing is as powerful as an idea whose time has come.
— Victor Hugo

Communication networks are becoming commonplace and are helping to change the face of research, development, production, and business. Local area networks and wide area networks are well established. Local area networks operate at high data rates with simple protocols; wide area networks operate at much lower speeds with relatively complex protocols.

On the one hand, the local area network (LAN) is used in connecting equipment owned by the same organization over relatively short distances. Its performance degrades as the area of coverage becomes large. Thus, LANs have limitations in geography, speed, traffic capacity, and the number of stations they are able to connect.

On the other hand, the wide area network (WAN) provides long-haul communication services to various points within a large geographical area—e.g., a continent. It is overkill for a modest community of users within a 25-km radius. Its limitations in serving a smaller area are due to such factors as history, design, cost, performance, and service types.

There is a need for an intermediate network that operates over a metropolitan area at comparatively high data rates and with reasonable protocol complexity. With some characteristics of LANs and some of WANs, the metropolitan area network (MAN) technology embraces the best features of both. The interconnection of LANs, MANs, and WANs is shown in Figure 1.1.

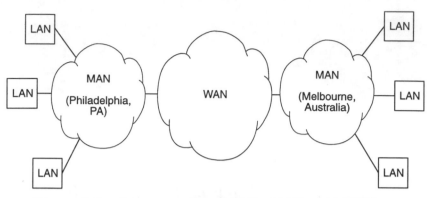

Figure 1.1   Interconnection of LANs, MANs, and WANs.

Metropolitan area networks are basically an outgrowth of LANs. The MAN effort was started in 1982, about two years after IEEE Project 802 was initiated [1]. The functional goals were to provide for interconnection of LANs, bulk data transfer, digitized voice, and video, as well as conventional terminal traffic. It was assumed that cable television (CATV), fiber optics, and radio were valid choices of media.

1.1 Definition of MAN

The term **MAN** is loosely defined; it means different things to different people. To most people, a MAN is a means of enabling diverse computing devices to communicate over high-speed links within a city-wide area. Some regard a MAN as a supernetwork that represents LAN technology optimized for the longer distances and using access protocols less sensitive to network size than those of LANs.

When a number of computer stations are distributed over a city, it is efficient to connect them in networks and then connect these networks by a high-speed network. (A high-speed system is one which operates at data rates exceeding 100 Mbps.) A metropolitan area network (MAN) is meant to accomplish the latter task.

The concept of a MAN is modeled after that of a LAN, operating at speeds of at least 10 Mbps, but applied to a larger geographical area (nominally 50 km in diameter). Typically, a MAN spans an entire office park, an entire campus, or an entire city and its suburbs. A MAN is therefore a high-speed network that interconnects a number of LANs, thereby allowing the sharing of resources and information within a metro community.

A MAN may also be regarded as a network that spans a larger geographical area than a LAN, but a smaller geographical area than a WAN.

1.2 Differences from LANs

A MAN performs like a LAN in that users cannot tell the difference in communicating across a room or across a city. Although the concept of a MAN is modeled after LAN principles, there are some major differences between the two types of networks. These differences can be summarized as follows [2, 3]:

- *Distance:* Whereas a LAN operates within a few kilometers, a MAN spans a city and its suburbs. IEEE Project 802 set a distance optimization of 50 km in diameter in order to match the dimensions of typical large metropolitan areas.

- *Backbone:* A backbone for interconnecting LANs is needed in a MAN to ease administration. The switching function is free; no large up-front expenditure for a switch is necessary in a shared-medium network.

- *Service:* Most of the traffic is digitized voice, not computer data. It is desirable that a MAN be optimized for carrying voice and video as well as computer data, thus having a more demanding access requirement. Voice has stringent requirements — a guaranteed bandwidth (64 kbps per voice channel) and bounded delay (2 μs at worst for round trip). These requirements for what are called isochronous channels cannot be met by conventional LANs.

- *Central Management:* A MAN requires central management for installation, operation, maintenance, and billing of users.

- *Public Operation:* A MAN is shared between many user organizations rather than being privately owned. This raises privacy and security issues in addition to requiring centralized operation and a need to gain right-of-way.

In a MAN, the speed of the backbone network is anticipated to be ten to a hundred times greater than that of a LAN. This speed disparity between the high-speed backbone and the lower-speed LANs that are connected to it creates a bottleneck situation at the gateways [4]. If, for example, we run our Ethernets at 10 Mbps, then interconnecting them at 10 kbps (a factor of 1000 less) surely results in bottlenecks. A control policy is necessary to regulate the flow of traffic, primarily that of traveling across the gateways from the backbone to the LANs.

1.3 Motivations for MAN

The motivations for MAN technology include the needs for (1) interconnection of LANs, (2) high-speed services, and (3) integrated services.

Interconnecting the LANs that are now commonplace in most work environments is necessary if the benefits of LANs are to be enhanced. A computer user connected to a LAN but separated from his host is currently forced to use a variety of measures to gain access to the host. These measures include several types of transmission media, ranging from modems to the use of a wide area network (assuming the host is connected to such a network) [5]. These measures have their own problems. Most links over modem occur at rates of 14 kbps or below. These links offer no integration of voice, video, and data streams. Using a WAN to connect a nearby host is inefficient because it involves using hundreds of kilometers of transmission which sometimes causes unacceptable delays. Thus the proliferation of LANs and the need for connection among the LANs have brought MANs to the fore.

The increasing customer demand for high-speed services has spawned the search for new technologies with wideband transport capabilities. Metropolitan area networks (MANs) are emerging as a possible candidate. MANs are public networks that are targeted to provide high-speed networking over metropolitan area distances. High-speed data communications have rapidly penetrated the workplace because of two complementary technological trends [6]:

- The availability of local area networks (LANs) that provide high-capacity, low-latency performance and a low per-port interconnection cost
- The dramatic, continuing decline in the cost of powerful computing devices

Most of the services of a MAN can be provided currently at low speeds but there is a definite demand for higher speed capabilities. For example, it is important that a travel agent get prompt responses from the host computer when making airline reservations. The salary of the agent depends on high speed data communication.

Current communication services are provided to users over dedicated access links for each network. This causes duplication of resources and inefficiency by dividing the traffic over a variety of media. It is advantageous for both operator and user to provide an integrated communication environment that can handle voice, video, and data simultaneously; new communication networks must be able to provide integrated services for users. However, different services have different network requirements. Data might be sensitive to loss, but the delay requirement might not be strict. On the other hand, voice traffic can accept a moderate loss but can tolerate only a limited delay.

MANs hold out promise for providing such integrated services.

1.4 Applications for MAN

A MAN is a high-speed communications network providing distributed switching between nodes for multiple services such as data, voice, and video over extended geographical areas. It allows effective customer access to the public network by integrating all end user services into a single customer access network.

There are two kinds of services MANs can provide. The first type is a broadband nonisochronous service over a metropolitan area. This service, known as *switched multi-megabit data service* (SMDS), is currently under development. The second type of service is to provide isochronous service (video and voice).

Areas where MANs can be used include the following:

- *LAN Interconnection:* extension of services offered by different autonomous LANs. MANs can interconnect LANs at remote sites within a metropolitan area. They can also provide gateway service to WANs and ISDNs.
- *Filetransfer:* electronic document exchange.
- *Distributed processing:* load sharing between several remote computers and common database access.
- *Remote Services:* software distribution and distributed backup.
- *Remote Login:* transparent access to a mainframe and video transmission.

1.5 Conclusion

The proliferation of LANs has necessitated their interconnection. This task is accomplished by MANs, which may be regarded as "composite LANs." MANs are metropolitan area–sized, high-speed, high-bandwidth networks.

The increasingly decentralized nature of businesses and their growing need to provide high-performance connectivity to distributed resources are some of the key factors that are driving the evolution towards MANs. As is shown in subsequent chapters, prototypes of MANs are already available. However, because technical problems and economic issues, the metropolitan area networks are yet to be fully implemented and commercialized.

References

[1] J. F. Mollenauer, "Metropolitan Area Networks: Where Many Standards Meet," *Proceedings of IEEE Computer Standard Conference,* 1988, pp. 2–6.

[2] ——, "Standards for Metropolitan Area Networks," *IEEE Communications Magazine,* vol. 26, no. 4, 1988, pp. 15–19.

[3] ——, "Metropolitan Area Networks and ATM Technology," *International Journal of Digital and Analog Cabled Systems,* vol. 1, no. 4, 1988, pp. 225–228.

[4] L. N. Wong and M. Schwartz, "Flow Control in Metropolitan Area Networks," *Proceedings of IEEE INFOCOM,* 1989, pp. 826–833.

[5] A. I. Karshmer, J. N. Thomas, and J. M. Phelan, "TVNet II: A Cable TV Based Metropolitan Area Networks Using the KEDS Protocol," *Microprocessing and Microprogramming*, vol. 30, no. 1–5, 1990, pp. 627–636.

[6] C. F. Hemrick, R. W. Klessig, and J. M. McRoberts, "Switched Multi-megabit Data Service and Early Availability via MAN Technology," *IEEE Communications Magazine*, vol. 26, no. 4, April 1988, pp. 9–14.

Chapter 2

MAN Technology

One machine can do the work of fifty ordinary men. No machine can do the work of one extraordinary man.

—Elbert G. Hubbard

The concept of a MAN can be discussed from several points of view. In this chapter, we discuss MAN architecture in the light of the OSI model, internetworking devices, and MAN topologies. Some of the key issues facing MAN technology are also addressed.

2.1 Protocol Architecture

The International Standards Organization (ISO) divides the task of networking computers into seven layers so that manufacturers can develop their own applications and implementations within the guidelines of each layer. The ISO developed a reference model, known as Open Systems Interconnection (OSI), which serves as a means of comparing different layers of communication networks. The seven layers of the OSI model are shown in Figure 2.1 and briefly explained as follows [1–3]:

- *Application Layer:* This layer is composed of specific application service elements, and its content varies with individual users. The layer is implemented with host software. Typical user programs include login, password check, electronic mailing system, bank balance, stock prices, credit check, inventory check, and airline reservation.

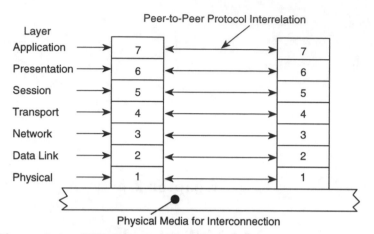

Figure 2.1 OSI Reference Model.

- *Presentation Layer:* This layer presents information in a way that is meaningful to the network user. It performs functions such as interpretation of character sets (e.g., ASCII, EBCDIC), conversion between character sets, data compression, data reformatting, and data encryption.
- *Session Layer:* A session is a connection between users. The session layer supervises sessions by establishing connection between users and managing the transfer of data between them.
- *Transport Layer:* This layer fragments messages into packets and reassembles the packets into messages. It also controls the end-to-end flow of packets, acknowledges successful transmission of packets, and requests retransmission of corrupted packets.
- *Network Layer:* This layer routes packets from their source to their destination and controls congestion. It carries addressing information that identifies the ultimate source and ultimate destination. It also counts transmitted bits for billing information.
- *Data Link Layer:* The purpose of this layer is to convert the bit pipe provided by the physical layer into a packet link, which is a facility for transmitting packets. In addition, this layer adds flags to indicate the beginning and the end of a message and adds check bits for detecting transmission errors. The layer is implemented in hardware. For LANs, the data link layer is decomposed into the media access control (MAC) and logical link control (LLC) sublayers.
- *Physical Link Layer:* This layer is responsible for converting raw bits into electrical (or optical) signal and transmitting them over a physical medium such a coaxial cable or an optical fiber.

Physically, a MAN consists of a transmission medium and nodes that provide customer access to the medium. Thus, a MAN consists of a medium and a MAC layer. In terms of protocol architecture, these fit into the OSI reference model as shown in Figure 2.2.

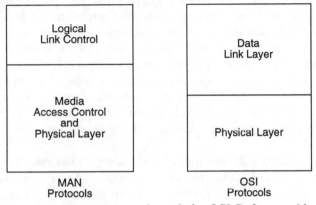

Figure 2.2   MAN Protocols and the OSI Reference Model.

2.2 Internetworking Devices

The subject of network interconnection (or internetworking) has generated a lot of interest, which can be attributed to the current proliferation of networks and a growing need for sharing resources and information among the networks. LAN interconnection is providing an impetus for the development of MAN. A review of literature of the entire field of network interconnection is provided by Biersack [4]. A similar review, strictly on LAN interconnection by MAN, is given by Cheng and Robertazzi [5]. The key works on network interconnection and protocol conversion are compiled by Green [6].

The primary purpose of internetworking is to enable a network user to establish communication link with the a user of another network and vice versa. Besides this, there are other scenarios that may require internetworking [7]:

- All LANs have a maximum number of stations they can support. If a user needs more stations on the network than is allowable, the only solution is to build multiple LANs and have them interconnected.
- By design a network may lack global coverage (e.g., a LAN). Users of this type of network may establish a communication link using an internetworking device.
- A new network may have limited service support capabilities and/or limited coverage in early stages.
- A particular network may be better suited to supporting a type of traffic generated by a user of another network.

- Computing resources may need to be shared among different sites belonging to the same organization.
- Teams working at different locations on the same project may need access to common data.

A metropolitan area network (MAN) may be viewed as an extension of a LAN to cover a metropolitan-sized area. Thus, a MAN is basically a network capable of providing high speed (greater than 10 Mbps) switched connectivity across distances typical of those found within a metropolitan area. To achieve the connectivity and facilitate communications between computer systems, network designers have implemented a number of interconnection devices: repeaters, routers, bridges, gateways, and, most recently, hybrid devices called brouters, trouters, and routing bridges [8–20]. The devices can be viewed in reference to the ISO model.

Interconnecting devices may operate at any of the seven layers of the OSI reference model. When connectivity between two systems is through an intermediary, the term *relay* is chosen to denote the intermediary in the ISO reference model. In the ISO terminology, a relay is known as a layer n relay if it shares a common layer n protocol with other systems but does not participate in a layer $n+1$ protocol in the relaying process [13].

- A repeater is a physical layer relay
- A bridge is a data link layer relay
- A router is a network layer relay
- A gateway is any higher layer than network layer relay.

It should be noted that these terms are used loosely in the marketplace. A vendor may call its product a "bridge" when it is capable of providing routing and protocol conversion.

2.2.1 Repeaters

Repeaters help overcome the electrical limits of a LAN — the limited length and the limited number of stations. A repeater is a physical layer device that receives, amplifies, and retransmits all incoming signals, including collisions. It simply forwards every packet from one network to the other. Thus, the repeater is only used to extend the length of the system, which is regarded as a single network. As a result, the collision mechanism applies and restricts the span of the network to about 2.5 km. Also, since the LANs are connected at the physical layer, as shown in Figure 2.3, each LAN shares the other's total traffic. This way, the efficiency and security of each LAN can be compromised. Bridges and gateways are more intelligent. These devices can filter intranetwork traffic and forward only internetwork packets.

2.2.2 Bridges

A bridge (also known as a data link relay) is a store-and-forward device that operates at the medium access control (MAC) layer. As a result, it can extend LANs far beyond the distance that repeaters can. It requires no address conversion because it interconnects LANs with a uniform address domain. In the majority of cases, bridges interconnect homogeneous or similar LANs (i.e. LANs with the same MAC Protocols). For example, a token bus bridge will interconnect two token bus LANs. The main attribute of bridges is transparency — a feature in a distributed system whereby users can access any local or remote resources just as if they were local. Bridges automatically initialize, configure themselves, and run with no intervention from network management.

Figure 2.3   Two LANs interconnected at the physical layer by a repeater.

A bridge is an intelligent device because it is capable of making decisions. It does this by referring to a table of addresses created for each LAN connected to the bridge. A bridge examines each packet as it passes, checking the source and destination addresses. If a packet coming from station 2 on LAN A is destined for station 5 on LAN A, the bridge allows the packet to move on. If the packet is destined for station 1 on LAN B, the bridge copies the packet onto LAN B. Thus, local traffic is kept on the LAN from which it originated and nonlocal traffic is forwarded to the appropriate destination.

Figure 2.4 shows two LANs interconnected using a MAC layer bridge. The major advantage of bridges is that they do not involve the end users in interconnecting LANs. They are self- learning and self-configuring. For a relatively small number of LANs with similar MAC protocols, such as the standard 802 LANs, a MAC bridge is perhaps the best approach because it is user transparent and requires the least processing time. One of their main disadvantages is that like other store-and-forward devices, bridges add to the total delay of a packet. This is undesirable for packets that have to make more than a few hops, as each bridge adds to the delay. Also, the performance of a bridge is limited by the rate at which it can examine incoming packets and decide whether a packet needs to be buffered and subsequently forwarded.

A bridge is subject to congestion. When congested, a bridge discards frames it cannot store. The end stations are responsible for the recovery of lost frames.

2.2.3 Routers

A router is a device that connects dissimilar networks and operates at the network layer in the OSI model. Its operation depends on the *internet protocol* (IP), a protocol at OSI layer 3. Consequently, it does not matter whether underlying networks are ethernet, token ring, or FDDI (fiber distributed data interface). This implies that routers accomodate a number of differences among networks. Such differences include different addressing schemes, routing techniques, maximum packet sizes, access controls, and error recovery.

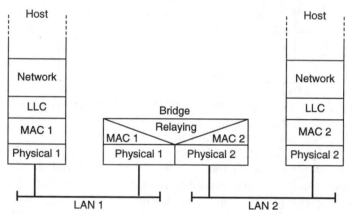

Figure 2.4   Two LANs interconnected at the data link layer by a bridge.

Routing is accomplished through a routing table at each end node. The routing table lists the various nodes on the network, the paths between the nodes, and how much it costs to transmit over those paths. Routing can be either static or dynamic. In static routing, once the routing table is configured by the network manager, the paths on the network never change. Although a static router issues an alarm, a dynamic router avoids portions of the network that are congested or have failed. A dynamic router will automatically reconfigure the routing table and recalculates the least expensive path when it recognizes that a particular link has gone down.

When a packet arrives, a router scans the destination address and looks it up in its routing table. If a particular node has more than one path, the router selects the most economical path. If the packet is larger than what the destination node would accept, the router breaks it down into a small size. As shown in Figure 2.5, routers process packets up to layer 3 and then forward them to a layer 3 function on the other LANs. The packets are then passed down the layers until finally transmitted. This causes delay. Thus, the routers work more slowly than repeaters and bridges. However, routers are more suited than bridges for some applications because routers implement layer 2 and 3 protocols. Also, because routers work at a higher level than bridges (which cover layers 1 and 2 of the OSI model), they provide end-user addressing. Like transparent bridges, they can also be used to connect two FDDI networks.

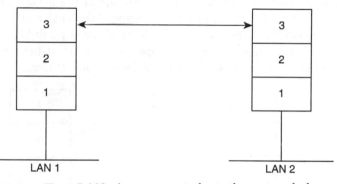

Figure 2.5 Two LANs interconnected at the network layer by a router.

A router is protocol dependent in that it connects logically separate networks operating under identical protocols. Routers are more sophisticated than bridges because routers must know each network's unique address when brought up and can select one of many possible paths to forward a packet based on a variety of parameters such as transit delay and congestion at other routers. Generally, routers provide a higher quality of service in their operation than do bridges. Quality of service is characterized by parameters such as availability, frame loss, transit delay, frame lifetime, undetected bit error rate, maximum supported frame size, and priority [17]. However, routers are inherently slower than bridges because they must determine which transport protocol is being used. Routers are useful in organizations with multiple large networks connected to a single backbone.

2.2.4 Gateways

When a device performs protocol conversions that enable information exchange among different types of networks, it is called a gateway. Gateways are used to connect LANs to other types of networks, particularly WANs. They act as translators between two inhomogeneous protocols. A gateway between networks receives messages from one network, translates them to a form that can be understood in the other network, and routes them to the appropriate destination [17]. It also translates names and addresses as necessary when messages are sent from one network to another. Thus, in addition to routing and flow control (as the bridge does), the gateway implements protocol conversion all the way up to OSI layer 7, particularly reformating the packets that go from one type of network to another. The amount and type of protocol conversion done by the gateway vary with the protocols and physical media of the networks involved. In addition, gateways act as buffers between networks with different transmission rates.

Like a router, a gateway performs routing at the network layer. As illustrated in Figure 2.6, gateways implement the entire protocol suite for each network. Depending on the level of incompatibility, gateways function at the transport through application layers of the OSI model. It is evident that gateways cause more delay than bridges and routers.

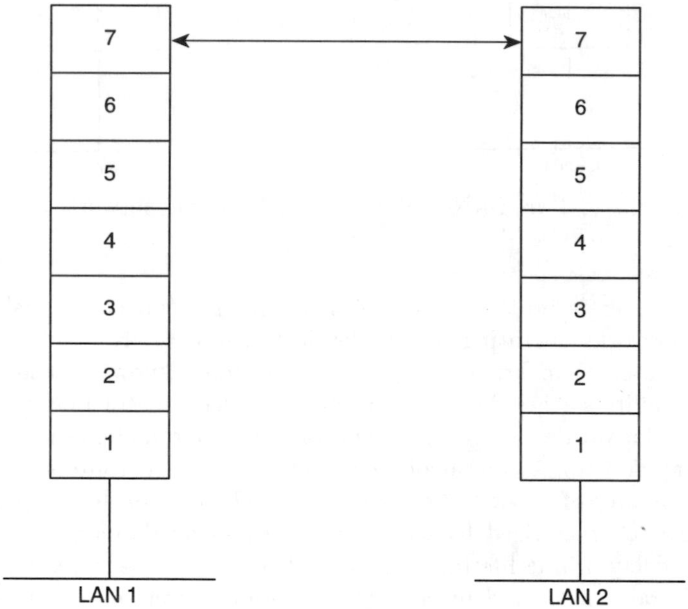

Figure 2.6   Two LANs interconnected at the equivalent of layer seven.

The difference between bridges and gateways becomes apparent as the number of active nodes increases. As illustrated in Figure 2.7, the processing time of the gateway does not increase if a hierarchical addressing scheme is properly used, whereas the processing time of a bridge is inversely proportional to the number of active nodes [12]. Thus, a gateway provides network management facilities essential for the successful deployment of large internets.

In a wide area networking environment, a gateway balances load levels, bypasses failed links, and finds the most economical route. Intelligent gateways capable of making decisions are being developed by some vendors. Such gateways can communicate with each other to decide the best way to route information, taking into account such factors as cost, security, congestion, throughput, delay, and error rate.

2.2.5 Hybrid Bridges and Routers

Some vendors have designed hybrid products that perform functions traditionally associated with the interconnecting devices just discussed. A gateway device, for example, may include some attributes of bridges and routers.

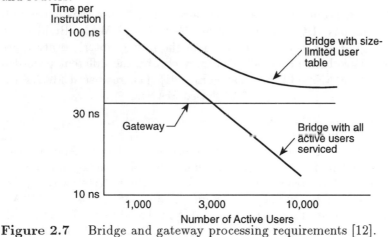

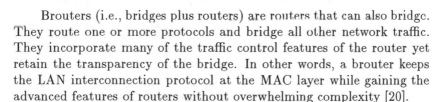

Figure 2.7   Bridge and gateway processing requirements [12].

Brouters (i.e., bridges plus routers) are routers that can also bridge. They route one or more protocols and bridge all other network traffic. They incorporate many of the traffic control features of the router yet retain the transparency of the bridge. In other words, a brouter keeps the LAN interconnection protocol at the MAC layer while gaining the advanced features of routers without overwhelming complexity [20].

A trouter is a combination of a router and a terminal server. It enables small work group 3s to connect to LANs, WANs, modems, printers, and other devices without having both a terminal server and a server.

Network interconnection involving repeaters, bridges, routers, and gateways have typically been designed in an ad hoc manner. With the ever increasing number of stations and corresponding increase in load, there is a need for a careful interconnection of the networks in order to extract the maximum benefits from the available resources.

One may view the relationship among relays as follows [13]:

1. Repeaters connect segments together to form a LAN.
2. Bridges connect LANs together to form a bridged network.
3. Level 1 routers connect bridged networks to form a level 1 network.
4. Level n $(n > 1)$ routers connect level $n - 1$ routers to form a level n network.

5. Gateways connect level n networks to form a "global" network.

In the future, broadband integrated service digital networks (B-ISDNs) will provide a means of internetworking LANs across a wide area. However, in using the B-ISDN to interconnect LANs, we must consider that support will be needed for existing ethernet and token ring LANs, high-speed LANs such as FDDI and DQDB (distributed-queue dual-bus), and supercomputer and ultragigabit LANs.

2.3 Topologies

The IEEE 802 committee has reached a consensus to use the distributed-queue dual-bus (DQDB) protocol as the standard MAN. Besides the IEEE DQDB MAN (to be discussed in the next chapter), other types of MAN have been proposed. One may classify the different proposed non-DQDB MANs into three categories [21]: (1) tree-based MANs, (2) toroid-based MANs, and (3) LAN-based MANs.

2.3.1 Tree-Based MANs

A tree has the most natural hierarchy because its components are also trees laid out in different levels. A binary tree offers the optimum solution in most data structures and search algorithms. Tree-based MANs have the same tree topology as community antenna television (CATV). Perhaps the greatest strength of using CATV-based networks is their almost universal existence in the United States. Roughly 60% of all homes are currently connected to a cable plant, and almost every building in most cities is passed by a cable [22].

In a tree-based MAN, stations are partitioned into subgroups. The subgroups are linked to the headend through hubs and subhubs, as shown in Figure 2.8. Two types of tree-based MANs have been proposed: those that use the CSMA/CD protocol and those that use a controlled access method called *group polling*. In the former types, stations in one subgroup contend for the channel by using a variation of the CSMA/CD protocol. Under the group polling scheme, the headend polls the subgroups in a cyclic manner [23, 24].

An advantage of a tree-based MAN is that it uses the minimum number of links to interconnect a set of points. Also, it can be implemented in an existing CATV network. Moreover, since the CATV network is essentially a broadband network, it provides several logical networks, each of which can be used in a manner that optimizes the performance of a particular application. A major drawback of the tree-based MAN is its reliability. The failure of the head brings the network down. Also, the failure of a hub or subhub disconnects a set of subgroups from the network. Other inherent problems in implementing tree-based MANs are discussed in Karshmer and Thomas [25] and by Karshmer, Thomas, and Phelan [26]. A solution of trading these disadvantages for a larger number of links has been found [27]. However, in view of these disadvantages, the possibility of seeing a tree-based MAN in the near future seems dim.

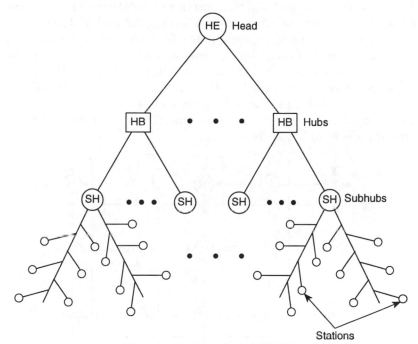

Figure 2.8 Tree-based MAN.

2.3.2 Toroid-Based MANs

Because of its structure, the toroidal network has held a fascination for communication and computer engineers. It provides an alternative to networks with linear topologies. It has multiple paths between sources and destinations that increase the reliability of the network and can be helpful in load balancing. The price of increased reliability and throughput is more complex routing and longer processing time at the nodes than in linear networks [28].

A two-dimensional toroidal network is a rectangular mesh where opposite nodes (or stations) on the left and right boundaries are connected to each other and opposite nodes on the upper and lower boundaries are also connected to each other [29]. The network has multiple paths between each source and destination pair thereby increasing the reliability of local networks. It consists of point-to-point links, and can be extended to cover a metropolitan area. Therefore, toroidal structures have been proposed as possible candidates for network interconnection [29–31]. There are at least four reasons for these proposals. First, toroidal networks are attractive because of their homogeneity, lack of boundaries, and Cartesian-like geometry. Second, the topology is isotropic; that is, every node has a similar set of connections to its neighbors. Third, addressing and routing is straightforward in a toroidal network. Moreover, for MANs the topology easily covers a rectangular grid of streets.

In a toroid-based MAN, each node represents a switching device to which are connected computing devices such as PCs, workstations, file servers, and hosts. A typical example of such a MAN is the Manhattan Street Network, where each link is unidirectional. Adjacent links, in both rows and columns, transmit packets in opposite directions. The end nodes of each row or column are connected via wraparound links as typically shown in Figure 2.9.

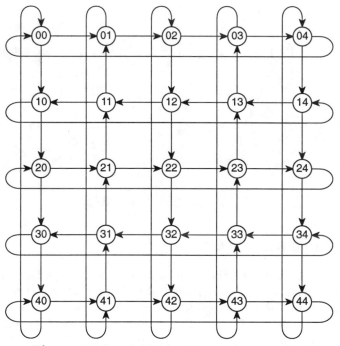

Figure 2.9 5 × 5 Manhattan street network.

One major advantage of the toroid-based MANs is their fault tolerance [21]. A fault-tolerant network has at least one redundant path between any pair of nodes. The redundant path is used to bypass a failed network component (link or node) on the primary path. This is in contrast to the tree-based network, where one link or node failure can disconnect a pair of users.

Other advantages of the toroidal topology include the same number of links per node, a symmetrical geometry, and a low maximal number of hops. The toroidal topology makes routing easy. It is also possible to add additional nodes and create hierarchies [29]. Toroidal networks increase the throughput of conventional local area networks by decreasing the fraction of the network capacity needed to transmit information between a source and a destination [30].

One disadvantage of the toroidal networks is that they require complex store-and-forward nodes that also route messages, control flow of data entering the network, resequence packets at the destination, and recover packets with error. However, there are characteristics of LANs or MANs that enable these functions to be simplified.

2.3.3 LAN-Based MANs

For LAN-based MANs, interconnection of the existing LANs is achieved either directly or through a backbone network [21].

A direct interconnection is made using a bridge or a gateway. Two homogeneous LANs (i.e., having the same access control (MAC) protocol) are connected with a bridge that performs routing and flow control functions. A gateway is used to connect two heterogeneous LANs. A typical example of direct interconnection of three bus and two ring LANs is shown in Figure 2.10. To eliminate the bottleneck problem of interconnecting high-speed LANs via bridges and gateways, interconnection via backbone networks has been proposed.

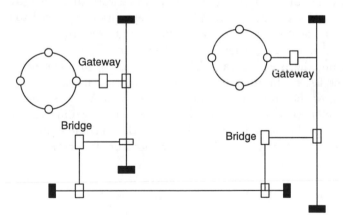

Figure 2.10   Direct interconnection of LANs using bridges and gateways.

Interconnection via a backbone network is achieved by means of either a broadcast network or a switched network. A broadcast network is one in which the stations in the network share a common transmission medium; data transmitted by one station is received by all the stations. Figures 2.11 and 2.12 illustrate LAN-based MANs with a backbone token ring network and a backbone CSMA/CD bus network, respectively. A typical example of a LAN-based MAN with a backbone network is the fiber distributed data interface (FDDI) network, which consists of an optical fiber token ring network as the backbone and a set of LANs accessing the backbone via bridges. The ring nature of FDDI provides a self-healing capability. However, the 100 Mbps speed is not compatible with synchronous optical networks (SONETs). This will initially prevent FDDI from spanning metropolitan areas and from providing voice communications. More will be said about FDDI in the next chapter.

The interconnection via a backbone, as typically shown in Figures. 2.11 and 2.12, offers superior performance to that of direct interconnection as in Figure 2.10 for the following reasons [21, 32].

- *Administration:* For ease of administration, it is better to use a backbone network scheme. It is easier to expand the network because existing LANs need not add new bridges each time another LAN is added to the network. Also, there are independent communication channels to prevent lockout by uncooperative networks or by network failures.

- *Traffic Regulation:* In an independent network, such as a MAN, it is easier to obtain global information to regulate traffic efficiently, to handle errors, and to control malicious traffic disruptions or illegal use of the network.

- *Cost:* The cost is comparable to other networks where the internetwork distance is larger than the intranetwork distance. Having a standard translation at a MAN node eliminates the need to rewrite the protocol software for each additional interconnection. Protocol conversion can be carried out in the backbone network, thus eliminating the need for each LAN to know the protocol used in the other LANs. In other words, a LAN does not have to know the protocols of others except the MAN it is connected to.

- *Security Reason:* A LAN owner may not be willing to accept en route traffic as well as go through other people's domain. The access to the MAN can be closely monitored at each of the nodes (or gateways).

The main disadvantage of a LAN-based MAN with a backbone concerns reliability; if the backbone fails, then inter-LAN communication is disrupted.

Beyond two or three LANs, the best interconnection method is to use a central switch [33–35]. A switched network consists of an interconnected system of nodes in which data are transferred from source to destination by being routed from one node to another. Since a switched network uses a different protocol from that of a LAN, all connections to a switched backbone network are made via a gateway.

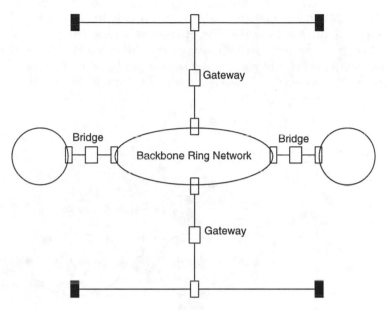

Figure 2.11 LAN-based MAN with a backbone ring network.

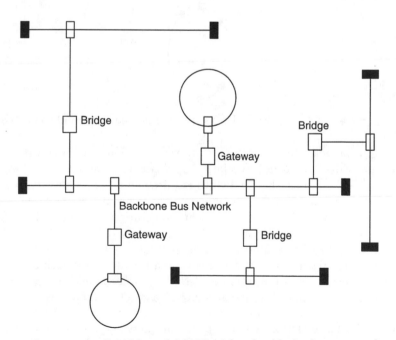

Figure 2.12 LAN-based MAN with a backbone bus network.

A large, almost unlimited, number of LANs can be interconnected with an ATM (asynchronous transfer mode) switch, as typically shown in Figure 2.13. ATM switches can operate at several hundred megabits per line at a very low cost by routing data through a switch a cell at a time [34]. Thus, tens of gigabits per second can be carried on the MAN, enough to provide for new services such as video telephony [33].

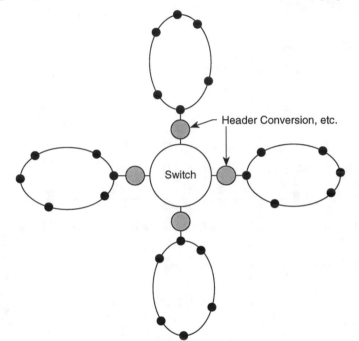

Figure 2.13 Multiple LANs interconnected by an ATM switch.

A major advantage of using such a system is that it allows for packet voice and video. A natural corollary of packetizing is compression, which can drastically reduce the bandwidth requirements. Consequently, compression opens the door to economical TV distribution by MAN. This is particularly interesting in the case of high-definition television (HDTV).

In addition, the switched backbone generally enhances the system reliability by providing alternate paths between every pair of stations in the network. It can span a wider area than a broadcast network because the latter has distance limitations. Also, the switched backbone network can interconnect more LANs than a broadcast network because there is a limit to the number of LANs that can be connected to the latter. A major drawback of the switched backbone network is that it is more expensive than the broadcast backbone network.

2.4 Key Issues

Although the metropolitan area network is closer to implementation to-day than it was several years ago, it has not yet realized its full potential because metropolitan area networks need to address problems that local area networks do not face. The key issues facing MANs include [25, 32, 36, 37]: (1) cost, (2) security, (3) reliability, (4) compatibility with current and future networks, (5) human factors, and (6) network management.

- *Cost:* Needless to say, cost and price are the major determining factors in the introduction of any new product or technology. The cost of a network is measured by such parameters as the total number of links (in a backbone network), bridges, gateways, and transceivers in the system [33]. The cost of connecting a network to a MAN, relative to the cost of the network itself, is an important issue from a user viewpoint. Connection cost includes both the cost of the electronic interface and the cost of the cable and its installation [27]. Because the cost per direct connection is very high, only the most powerful devices are costly enough to justify direct connection to a MAN. Low-speed, low-cost devices neither need nor can afford a direct connection to a high-speed medium. Hence, at least a two-level hierarchy of networks is needed. A low-speed device (e.g. 5 Mbps) is connected along with other similar devices to a low-cost network that is then connected to a high-speed (e.g. 100 Mbps) backbone network via a bridge. Because many organizations already have more than one LAN, the most common approach to building a MAN is the interconnection of LANs; it is more economical to interconnect them than to build a network that will serve the same purpose.

- *Security:* Security is an issue because MANs will likely be owned and operated by common carriers, rather than being privately owned. No customer will be satisfied with his confidential data passing through a competitor's stations, and no operator will be pleased with a network in which one customer could disrupt the service of others, either accidentally or maliciously. Thus, privacy, protection against unauthorized access, and correct billing must be ensured. These problems are not faced with LANs, which are typically owned and operated by the same organization that uses them. However, MANs as public networks can probably provide better security for the cost than anyone else.

- *Reliability:* The reliability issue concerns two basic functions: transmission and routing. The transmission function relies on both the integration of the transmission media and the correct operation of the access protocols, whereas the reliability of the routing function depends on the reliability of bridges and gateways. A failure in a bridge may isolate a LAN. However, each of the resulting networks is not affected in its internal communications. With the aid of optical directional couplers, a fiber-optic MAN can be constructed whose reliability equals, if not exceeds, that obtained in hierarchical structures.

- *Compatibility:* Compatibility with existing and future networks is an important issue. Much care has gone into providing good compatibility between the 802.6 standard and new standards for wide area networking. For example, telephone companies have established certain quality goals for their digital transmission systems in support of the integrated services digital networks (ISDN). Any MAN being used for telephone should act as an extension of the ISDN and so should meet these quality goals as well [38]. Thus the proposed MANs are compatible with ISDN. In particular, the new broadband ISDN (BISDN) is ideal for interconnecting MANs. More about ISDN is covered in Chapter 4.

- *Human Factors:* Human factors such as user friendliness and user adaptability are crucial. Educating the service provider and potential customers is an important strategy. In order to provide a MAN, a company would have to be attuned to what customer's needs are and how to meet them. New services would have to be developed to aid customers and show them how to benefit from these new services.

- *Network Management:* The network must have the capability of customer network management. A MAN requires a central organization to install it, operate it, and bill users for services. The network management is responsible for evaluating customer utilization of network resources and services in order to charge the proper bill to each customer. The services offered by MANs necessitate the need to revise the present charging and tariffing methods for connection-oriented services [39]. For ease of administration, it may be expedient to use the scheme with a backbone network.

Although some of these issues are interrelated, they are the major factors that can influence the choice of schemes. The issues are holding back MANs from realizing their full potential and must be addressed in implementing MANs. Any MAN service must offer capabilities to address these and other related issues.

2.5 Conclusion

In this chapter, we have discussed MAN technology from different perspectives. A MAN has been viewed as a composite LAN—i.e., a direct interconnection of LANs via repeaters, routers, bridges, and gateways. These internetworking devices provide varying levels of connectivity, efficiency, and economy to corporate networking. The choice of a particular device depends largely on the topology of the networks under consideration and the types of applications being run on the networks.

A MAN may also be viewed as an indirect interconnection of LANs via a backbone through either a broadcast network or a switched network.

We also mentioned some key issues facing MANs. Such issues include the cost of the network, its security and reliability, its compatibility with current and future networks, and management problems. Such issues can put a premium on MAN. This notwithstanding, several proposals on MAN protocols and topologies have been made and implemented. Some of these proposals are covered in the next chapter.

References

[1] A. S. Tanenbaum, *Computer Networks*. Englewood Cliffs, NJ: Prentice-Hall, 1989.

[2] J. Walrand, *Communication Networks: A First Course*. Boston, MA: Irwin, 1991.

[3] C. Panasuk, "Designer's Reference," *Electronic Design*, Dec. 27, 1984, pp. 87–94.

[4] E. W. Biersack, "Annotated Bibliography on Network Interconnection," *IEEE Journal Selected Areas in Communications*, vol. 8, no. 1, Jan. 1990, pp. 22–41.

[5] Y. C. Cheng and T. G. Robertazzi, "Annotated Bibliography of Local Communication System Interconnection," *IEEE Journal Selected Areas in Communications*, vol. 5, no. 9, Dec. 1987, pp. 1492–1499.

[6] P. E. Green, *Network Interconnection and Protocol Conversion*. New York: IEEE Press, 1988.

[7] S. L. Sutherland and J. Burgin, "B-ISDN Internetworking," *IEEE Communications Magazine*, Aug. 1993, pp. 60–63.

[8] P. Schnaidt, *LAN Tutorial*. San Francisco, CA: Miller Freeman Publications, 1990, pp. 89–109.

[9] R. C. Dixon and D. A. Pitt, "Addressing, Bridging, and Source Routing," *IEEE Network*, vol. 2, no.1, Jan. 1988, pp. 25–32.

[10] W. M. Seifert, "Bridges and Routers," *IEEE Network*, vol. 2, no. 1, Jan. 1988, pp. 57–64.

[11] M. Gerla and L. Kleinrock, "Congestion Control in Interconnected LANs," *IEEE Network*, vol. 2, no. 1, Jan. 1988, pp. 72–76.

[12] H. Salwen, R. Boule, and J. N. Chiappa, "Examination of the Applicability of Router and Bridging Techniques," *IEEE Network*, vol. 2, no.1, Jan. 1988, pp. 77–80.

[13] R. Perlman, A. Harvey, and G. Varghese, "Choosing the Appropriate ISO Layer for LAN Interconnection," *IEEE Network*, vol. 2, no.1, Jan. 1988, pp. 81–86.

[14] W. Bauerfeld, "A Tutorial on Network Gateways and Interworking of LANs and WANs," *Computer Networks and ISDN Systems*, vol. 13, 1987, pp. 187–193.

[15] N. Linge *et al.*, "A Bridge Protocol for Creating a Spanning Tree Topology within an IEEE 802 Extended LAN Environment," *Computer Networks and ISDN Systems*, vol. 13, 1987, pp. 323–332.

[16] F. Fluckiger, "Gateways and Converters in Computer Networks," *Computer Networks and ISDN Systems*, vol. 16, 1988/89, pp. 55–59.

[17] J. H. Benjamin *et al.*, "Interconnecting SNA Networks," *IBM Systems Journal*, vol. 22, no. 4, 1983, pp. 344–366. Also in P. E. Green [6], pp. 51–72.

[18] E. Ball *et al.*, "Local Area Network Bridges," *Computer Communications*, vol. 11, no. 3, June 1988, pp. 115–118.

[19] J. A. Berntsen, *et al.*, "MAC Layer Interconnection of IEEE 802 Local Area Networks," *Computer Networks and ISDN Systems*, vol. 10, no. 5, 1985, pp. 259–273.

[20] Y. D. Lin and M. Gerla, "Brouter: The Transparent Bridge with Shortest Path in Interconnected LANs," *Proceedings of IEEE 16th Conference on Local Computer Networks*, 1991, pp. 175–183.

[21] O. C. Ibe and R. C. Howe, "Architectures for Metropolitan Area Networks," *Computer Communications*, vol. 12, no. 6, Dec. 1989, pp. 315–323.

[22] A. I. Karshmer and R. Yan, "A Cable TV Based Metropolitan Area Network Using Distributed Switching," *Microprocessing and Microprogramming*, 1993, vol. 37, pp. 197–200.

[23] O. C. Ibe, "An Integrated CATV-Type Metropolitan Area Network," *Computer Networks and ISDN Systems*, vol. 13, 1987, pp. 291–299.

[24] O. C. Ibe and X. Cheng, "A Medium Access Control Protocol for CATV-Type Networks," *Proceedings of IEEE INFOCOM*, 1987, pp. 150–154.

[25] A. I. Karshmer and J. N. Thomas, "Inherent Problems in Implementing Cable TV Based Metropolitan Area Networks," *Proceedings of the 22nd Annual Hawaii International Conference on System Sciences*, 1989, vol. IV, pp. 338–347.

[26] A. I. Karshmer, J. N. Thomas, and J. M. Phelan, "TVNet II: A Cable TV Based Metropolitan Area Network Using the KEDS Protocol," *Microprocessing and Microprogramming*, 1990, vol. 30, no. 1-5, pp. 627–635.

[27] J. W. Mark and O. W. W. Yang, "Design and Analysis of a Metropolitan Area Network: A Two-Center Tree Net," *Proceedings of Computer Networking Symposium*, 1986, pp. 46–54.

[28] R. Krishman and N. F. Maxemchuk, "Life Beyond Linear Topologies," *IEEE Network*, March 1993, pp. 48–54.

[29] T. G. Robertazzi, "Toroidal Networks," *IEEE Communications Magazine*, vol. 26, no. 6, June 1988, pp. 45–50.

[30] N. F. Maxemchuk, "Regular Mesh Topologies in Local and Metropolitan Area Networks," *AT & T Technical Journal,* vol. 64, no. 7, Sept. 1985, pp. 1659–1685.

[31] ——, "Routing in the Manhattan Street Network," *IEEE Transactions on Communications,* vol. 35, no. 5, May 1987, pp. 503–512.

[32] O. W. W. Yang and J. W. Mark, "Design Issues in Metropolitan Area Networks," *Proceedings of IEEE International Conference on Communications (ICC '86)*, pp. 899–903.

[33] J. F. Mollenauer, "Metropolitan Area Networks and ATM Technology," *International Journal of Digital and Analog Cabled Systems*, vol. 1, no. 4, 1988, pp. 225–228.

[34] A. Pattavina, "Performance Evaluation of ATM Switches with Input and Output Queuing," *International Journal of Digital and Analog Cabled Systems*, vol. 3, no. 3, 1990, pp. 227–286.

[35] J. F. Mollenauer, "Metropolitan Area Networks: A New Application for Fiber," *Photonics Spectra*, vol. 24, no. 3, 1990, pp. 159–161.

[36] T. I. Bajenescu, "High Speed Optical MAN Integrating Voice, Video and Data Switching," *Proceedings of IEEE International Conference on Communications (ICC '90)*, pp. 675–679.

[37] C. J. Cranfill, "Issues in Implementing a Public Metropolitan Area Network," *Proceedings of IEEE International Conference on Communications (ICC '90)*, pp. 1572–1575.

[38] D. T. W. Sze, "A Metropolitan Area Network," *IEEE Journal on Selected Areas in Communications*, vol. SAC-3, no.6, 1985, pp. 815–824.

[39] G. Bottura, "Charging and Tariffing Functions and Capabilities for MANs," *Proceedings of IEEE Network Operations and Management Symposium*, 1992, vol.1, pp. 208–218.

Chapter 3

Proposed MANs

Skepticism has never founded empires, established principles or changed the world's heart. The great doers in history have always been men of faith.

—Edwin H. Chapin

The last ten years have witnessed a proliferation of proposals for high-speed local area networks (LANs) and metropolitan area networks (MANs). The development of MANs is following a similar trend to that of LANs. Unlike LANs, however, designing MANs poses some challenging problems. Such problems include the following [1]:

- Support of a large number of stations
- Coverage of a large geographical area
- Real-time traffic (voice, video) support
- Very high bandwidth requirements

Like LANs, additional requirements in designing MANs include high availability, growth flexibility, and fault tolerance. Of course, the overriding criterion that must be met by any proposal is its economic viability. To meet these and other requirements, several proposals have been made for MAN protocols and architectures.

This chapter presents some MAC protocols proposed for metropolitan area networks. Expressnet and Fasnet are first discussed briefly (in Sections 3.1 and 3.2, respectively) because they were among the first set of protocols to be proposed in this field. The two networks suffer limitations in the number of stations that can be connected. FDDI, the most popular example of an extended LAN, and DQDB, the IEEE standard protocol for MANs, are discussed at a greater depth in Sections 3.3 and 3.4, respectively. FDDI and DQDB are the two emerging standards that compete for use as backbones. The two standards are compared in

Section 3.5; their detailed performance analysis is delayed until the next chapter. Some other proposed MANs are discussed briefly in Section 3.6.

3.1 Expressnet

The Expressnet was originally proposed as a broadcast network based on a unidirectional fiber-optic folded bus [2–4]. The transmission medium consists of two main channels, the inbound or read (R) channel and the outbound or write (W) channel, to which the stations are connected as shown in Figure 3.1. The channels are joined so that all signals transmitted on the W channel are duplicated on the R channel, thus achieving broadcast communication among the stations. As shown in Figure 3.2, each station is connected to the bus through three unidirectional taps: a write tap in the W channel, a sense (S) tap to sense upstream activity on the W channel, and a read tap in the R channel. In order to transmit on the bus, the stations utilize a distributed access protocol, which achieves a conflict-free round-robin scheduling.

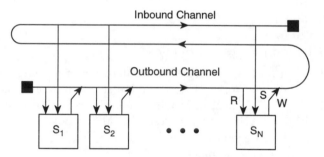

Figure 3.1 Topology of Expressnet.

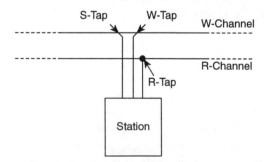

Figure 3.2 Expressnet taps.

The Expressnet MAC protocol uses an implicit token algorithm; that is, stations recognize their turn for transmission by detecting special events on the bus. A station contends for the channel as follows:

1. It waits for the end of carrier (EOC) code on the W channel.
2. Upon detecting EOC on the S tap of the W channel, it starts transmitting and continues to sense the upstream activity on the S tap.
3. If activity is detected from upstream, it aborts the transmission and the procedure is repeated. Otherwise, it completes the transmission.

The most upstream station can transmit with no fear of interference, but all other stations may interfere with the stations upstream. Stations are allowed at most one packet transmission per train. The protocol can be extended to allow integration of isochronous and bursty traffic by constraining the train length and alternating different types of trains on the bus. The main causes of performance degradation in Expressnet are the time the channel remains idle between two cycles (order of the end-to-end propagation delay), the overhead in each cycle, and the headers in front of every packet. Since the protocol is asynchronous, packets require a synchronization preamble, which can be fairly long at high data rates.

ExpressMAN is a metropolitan area network architecture based on the Expressnet access mechanism [5]. It uses Expressnet as both local and backbone networks. As shown in Figure 3.3, the stations are attached to the local buses as in Expressnet, and the local buses are connected to the backbone via local control units that act as switching units. The overall network structure is halfway between a linear bus and a two-level hierarchical structure in which several subnetworks are connected by a backbone network. It is a broadcast network and does not require routing facilities such as bridges.

A major advantage of Expressnet is that it achieves high utilization, especially when the number of backlogged stations is large. This makes Expressnet suitable for high-speed operations. A major disadvantage is the complexity of its access protocol, which may lead to high costs of implementation.

3.2 Fasnet

Fasnet [4, 6–8] adopts a dual-bus topology, as shown in Figure 3.4. It is designed to multiplex voice and data traffic onto a local area network of two unidirectional transmission lines. Each station is connected to two identical unidirectional buses where the signals propagate in opposite directions. Also, each station has two sets of read and write connections for sensing and transmitting, respectively, on the line.

The Fasnet MAC protocol uses a slotted access algorithm with an implicit token behavior. Its operation is synchronous, with time divided into slots. Packets may have to be fragmented in order to fit the slots. To ensure fairness, Fasnet operates in cycles. This way all stations are permitted to transmit a given number of fixed-length packets during a cycle. A new cycle begins only after all stations have been permitted to transmit. Cycles are initiated by the most upstream station (station 1 for bus A in Figure 3.4). This station also generates a succession of slots, whose format is shown in Figure 3.5. Each slot begins with an access control field (ACF), which determines how and when each station may access the channel. The ACF consists of three bits: The start bit (SB), when set, denotes the start of a new cycle; the busy bit (BB), when set, shows that a packet has been written into the slot; and the end bit (EB), when set, instructs the most upstream station to start a new cycle on the other channel.

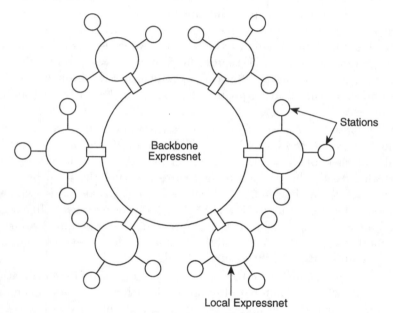

Figure 3.3 ExpressMAN topology.

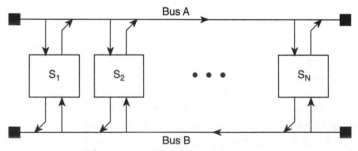

Figure 3.4 Topology of Fasnet.

The operation of the two buses is identical. If a station wants to transmit a packet, it must first sense the bus by means of a nondirectional tap. It then transmits on the channel that has the recipient downstream. This means that each station must know the relative location of other stations in the network. The end station (the most downstream station) detects the end of transmission of all ready stations in the current cycle. After transmitting in a given frame, a station has to wait for the next start of cycle (when SB = 1) for its next transmission. This way, fairness to all stations is ensured. However, a priority station may transmit several packets in consecutive slots up to some maximum value.

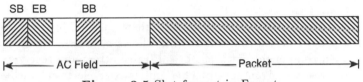

Figure 3.5 Slot format in Fasnet.

Fasnet achieves higher aggregate channel throughput than Expressnet because of the capability of two concurrent transmissions on the two buses. This does not come for free, of course. It is gained at the expense of requiring that the stations have the knowledge of the relative location of other stations connected to the buses. From a performance standpoint, shorter paths can be expected for data transmission.

An irregular pattern of cycle lengths and unfairness among users is exhibited in Fasnet. Preference is given to upstream users. The main causes of performance degradation in Fasnet are the time the channel remains idle between cycles (order of end-to-end delay), the overhead in each slot, and the possible partial filling of slots due to variable packet size. The integration of different types of traffic can be obtained by using more than one bit for the start of cycle, encoding the type of traffic to which the cycle refers.

3.3 FDDI

In the mid-1970s, it was recognized that the existing copper technology would be unsuitable for future communication networks. In view of this, the telecommunication industry invested heavily in research into optical fibers. Optical fibers offer some benefits over copper in that they are essentially immune to electromagnetic interference (EMI), have low weight, do not radiate, and reduce electrical safety concerns.

The fiber distributed data interface (FDDI) is proposed by the American National Standard Institute (ANSI) as a dual token ring that supports data rates of 100 Mbps and uses optical fiber media [9–16]. Optical fiber is used as the transmission medium in FDDI for the following reasons [12, 14]:

- *Bandwidth:* It provides a very high capacity for carrying information. It has sufficient bandwidth that bit-serial transmission can be

used, thereby considerably reducing the size, cost, and complexity
of the hardware.

- *Attenuation:* It provides low attenuation and is therefore capable
  of transmitting over a long distance without the need of repeaters.
- *Noise Susceptibility:* It neither radiates nor is affected by electromagnetic interference.
- *Security:* It is more secure from malicious interception because it is
  not easy to tap a fiber-optic cable without interrupting communication.
- *Cost:* The cost of optical fibers has fallen considerably over the last
  few years and will continue to fall. The same is true for the cost of
  related components such as optical transmitters and receivers.

These impressive advantages of fiber optics over electrical media and
the inherent advantages of a ring design contribute to the widespread
acceptance of FDDI as a standard. Although the FDDI MAC protocol
is similar to IEEE 802.5, there are some differences. Some of these
differences are summarized in Table 3.1.

Table 3.1   Differences between FDDI and IEEE 802.5.

FDDI	IEEE 802.5
100 Mbps	4, 16 Mbps
Optical fiber	Shielded twisted pair
Half-duplex architecture	Full-duplex architecture
Reliability specification	None
Group encoding	Differential Manchester
Limited packet size	Packets can be very long
Distributed clocking	Centralized clocking
Traffic regulated through timed token	Traffic regulated through priority and reservation bits
New token after transmit	New token after receive

3.3.1 Basic Features

FDDI is both an interface technology and a protocol. The two main
attributes of FDDI are its size and transmission rates. It operates at
100 Mbps and can connect as many as 500 nodes per ring, with up to 2
kilometers between nodes and a total LAN circumference of about 100
km. FDDI is therefore classified as a MAN as well as a LAN.

FDDI can be configured into a variety of topologies including dual
ring with or without trees, wrapped ring with or without trees, and
single tree. Figure 3.6 shows the most general FDDI topology (known
as *a ring of trees*, where each tree denotes a subsection of the network).

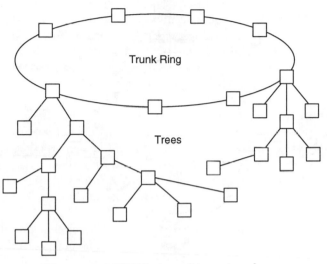

Figure 3.6 FDDI ring-of-trees topology.

As shown in Figure 3.7, each FDDI station is connected to two rings, primary and secondary. Stations have active taps on the ring and operate as repeaters. This is what allows an FDDI network to be so large without signal degradation. The network uses its primary ring for data transmission and the secondary ring either to ensure fault tolerance or for data. When a station or link fails, the primary and secondary rings form a single one-way ring, isolating the fault while maintaining a logical path among users, as shown in Figure 3.8. Thus, FDDI's dual-ring topology and connection management functions establish a fault-tolerance mechanism.

Like a token ring LAN, access to the network in FDDI is gained by capturing a circulating token, a short packet which is the transmission permit. When a station has a packet for transmission, it waits for a token. On receiving a token, the station transmits its packet before inserting the token in the ring again. The station passes on the token immediately after transmitting the message and *before* receiving an acknowledgment that the message has been received. (Thus, unlike token ring LANs, packets from several stations can share the ring simultaneously. Also, because of the high data rate, it would be grossly inefficient to require stations to wait for their message to return, as in regular token ring LANs. This slight change in the protocol avoids wasting bandwidth.) All stations circulate the transmitted packet along the ring until it reaches its source station, where it is extracted from the ring.

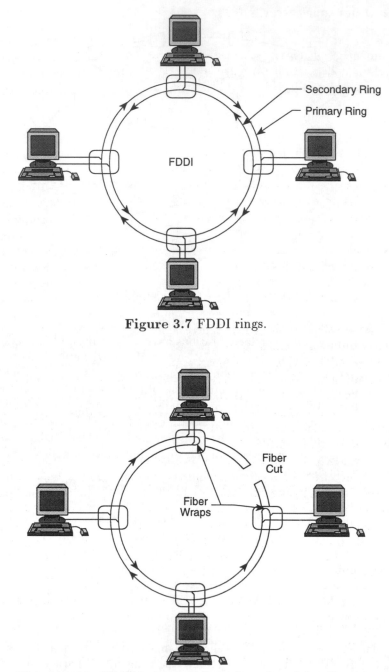

Figure 3.7 FDDI rings.

Figure 3.8   FDDI isolates fault without impairing the network.

3.3.2 Architecture

FDDI was developed to conform with the OSI reference model. Architecturally, an FDDI station consists of four standardized layers:

- PMD: The physical-medium-dependent (or media) layer, which provides the electrical or optical link connection to the FDDI ring. PMD options include single-mode/multimode optical fiber, unshielded/shielded twisted-pair copper wire, and synchronous optical network (SONET). The PMD layer specifies full-duplex connectors, optical transceivers, and bypass switches (optional).
- PHY: The physical (or signal) layer, which interfaces to PMD and handles encoding and decoding of information. It specifies a set of line states that perform a handshake between PHYs in adjacent stations. It uses a distributed clocking scheme to maintain ring synchronization at the physical level.
- MAC: The media access control (or access) layer, which connects PHY to higher OSI layers and handles functions such as data transfer, ring recovery, and group addressing.
- STM: The station management (or network management) layer, which controls the other three layers and ensures proper operation of the station. It handles such functions as station initialization, station insertion and removal, activation, connection management, address administration, monitoring, scheduling policies, collection of statistics, bandwidth allocation, fault detection and isolation, and ring reconfiguration.

The complete architecture is shown in Figure 3.9. A comparison of the FDDI architectural model to the lower two layers of the OSI model is shown in Figure 3.10.

3.3.3 Data Units

FDDI packets are called *frames.* On the FDDI ring, information is transmitted in frames, which are variable in length. The frames are self-defining in that each frame contains delimiters that mark its beginning and end. The logical link control supplies MAC with a service data unit, which is encapsulated into a frame for transmission by the physical medium. Data is transferred across the PHY-to-MAC interface in terms of two kinds of symbols: data symbols and control symbols. Each symbol requires 5 code bits for its transfer onto the fiber-optic medium [17, 18].

Due to the optical medium, the FDDI physical layer uses a two-stage coding scheme for every symbol passed down from the MAC. The first coding stage converts the symbol to 5 NRZ (nonreturn to zero) code bits using the 4B/5B (4 out of 5) scheme, shown in Table 3.2. The scheme allows 4-bit data to be encoded into 5 bits for transmission.

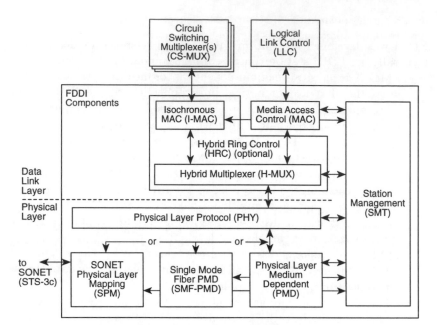

Figure 3.9 FDDI architecture.

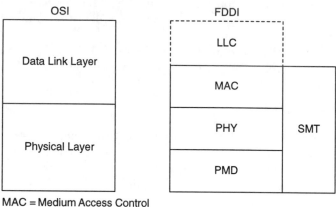

MAC = Medium Access Control
PHY = Physical Layer
PMD = Physical Medium Dependent
SMT = Station Management

Figure 3.10　Comparison of OSI and FDDI models.

Since a 4-bit data packet is changed into a 5-bit symbol, the 4B/5B encoding scheme has an 80% efficiency and the 100-Mbps date rate necessitates a 125-MHz clock. The second coding stage converts the NRZ bits into an NRZI (nonreturn to zero invert on ones) bit stream. Figure 3.11 shows a typical example of two 4B/5B symbols being converted to NRZ, then to NRZI.

Table 3.2   4B/5B Symbol Coding.

Decimal	Code	Symbol	Name	Assignment
00	00000	Q	Quiet	Line state symbol
31	11111	I	Idle	" " "
04	00100	H	Halt	" " "
24	11000	J		Starting delimiter
17	10001	K		" "
05	00101	L		" "
13	01101	T		Ending delimiter
07	00111	R	Reset	Control indicator
25	11001	S	Set	" "
30	11110	0		Data symbol 0000
09	01001	1		" " 0001
20	10100	2		" " 0010
21	10101	3		" " 0011
10	01010	4		" " 0100
11	01011	5		" " 0101
14	01110	6		" " 0110
15	01111	7		" " 0111
18	10010	8		" " 1000
19	10011	9		" " 1001
22	10110	A		" " 1010
23	10111	B		" " 1011
26	11010	C		" " 1100
27	11011	D		" " 1101
28	11100	E		" " 1110
29	11101	F		" " 1111
01	00001	V	Violation	Not transmitted
02	00010	V	Violation	" "
03	00011	V	Violation	" "
06	00110	V	Violation	" "
08	01000	V	Violation	" "
12	01100	V	Violation	" "
16	10000	V	Violation	" "

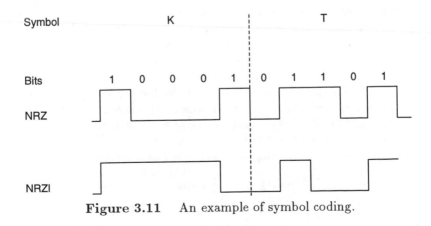

Figure 3.11   An example of symbol coding.

The 5-bit symbols shown in Table 3.2 provide 32 possible bit combinations. Ten of these combinations violate the run length and direct current balance requirement, however, leaving 22 code groups that can appear on the ring during normal operations. Sixteen code groups represent data values; the remaining six are control symbols, such as those delimiting the beginning and end of packets. The quiet, halt, and idle symbols are line state symbols. (The line states are used to indicate the condition of the physcial link and to signal for link control functions.) The quiet (Q) symbol denotes the absence of any functional signal; the halt (H) symbol indicates a forced logical break in activity or the removal of code violation symbols; the idle (I) symbol is used to indicated that there are no MAC transmissions. The JK symbol pair is used as the starting delimiter field designating the beginning of a frame. The L symbol is used only in FDDI-II for imbedding the MAC starting delimiter within the cycle structure. The R and S symbols are used as control indicators. The reset symbol R indicates a logical 0 or reset condition, and the set symbol S denotes a logical 1 or set condition. The terminate symbol T is used for ending delimiters.

3.3.4 Frame and Token Formats

The basic data link frame structure for FDDI is similar to that specified for IEEE 802 frames, with the exception of starting and ending delimiters. The maximum frame length is 9,000 bytes; data packets can range from 128 bytes to 4,500 bytes. This makes FDDI ideal for large file transfer.

Figure 3.12 shows the formats of the frame and token used by FDDI. The frame or token contains symbols, with each representing 4 bits of information. The preamble (PA) precedes every transmission and synchronizes the packet with each station's clock. The starting delimiter (SD) indicates the beginning of the packet. The frame control (FC) signifies the type of packet (token or data) and its characteristics (synchronous or asynchronous, MAC, LLC, or SMT). The FC field distinguishes between two kinds of tokens: restricted and nonrestricted. The restricted token keeps other stations off the network while a high priority task is performed. The end delimiter (ED) completes the packet. Data packets also contain a source address (SA), a destination address (DA), and an information field (DATA), a frame check sequence (FCS), and a frame status (FS) field. The frame check sequence (FCS) is a cyclic redundance check using the ANSI standard polynomial. The frame status (FS) field is used for a station to indicate it has detected an error.

3.3.5 Access and Priority Mechanism

The FDDI MAC uses a timed token-rotation (TTR) protocol for controlling access to the medium. With this protocol, the MAC in each station measures the time that has elapsed since the station last received a token. The use of the TTR protocol allows stations to request establish guaranteed bandwidth and response time for synchronous frames. It also establishes a maximum ring utilization equal to

$$\rho_{\max} = \frac{\text{TRT} - \text{RL}}{\text{TRT}} \tag{3.1}$$

where RL is the physical ring latency, the time for a token to go around an idle ring.

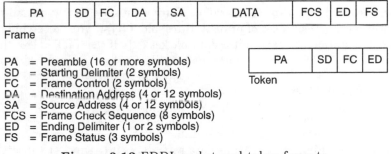

Figure 3.12 FDDI packet and token formats.

During initialization, all stations negotiate for a target token-rotation time (TTRT). This TTRT value is set equal to the value of the token-rotation time (TRT), which is used to monitor the time elapsed between subsequent arrivals of token at the station. When running, the TRT counts down to zero. If a token arrives before TRT expires, the token is said to be early. Under this situation, the station is permitted to send asynchronous frames for an amount of time that equals the earliness of the token. If the token arrives after TRT expires, it is said to be late and the station is not allowed to send any asychronous frames. A token will arrive on the average of every TTRT seconds although it may arrive early or late on any given rotation. The TTRT value is selected so that the average TRT $\leq$ TTRT and the maximum TRT $\leq 2 \times$ TTRT.

The FDDI standard is designed to allow a wide range of traffic simultaneously by means of a timer-based priority mechanism. FDDI supports two major classes of traffic: synchronous traffic and asynchronous traffic. The synchronous class provides a guaranteed bandwidth for time-critical messages such as voice and video signals. The remaining bandwidth is dynamically allocated among asynchronous traffic, which holds messages such as data that have no real- time requirement. The transmission of frames in the asynchronous traffic class can be based on two token modes. Using the unrestricted token, up to eight priority levels can be distinguished. A restricted token mode in the asynchronous traffic class allows dialog-oriented connections between two nodes.

The token holding timer (THT) is used by every station to control the amount of time a station may transmit asychronous frames. If the token is not late, the value of THT does not start timing until the transmission of the synchronous frames has been completed. The transmission of isochronous frames in each station is controlled by a synchronous holding timer. The transmission of isochronous frames is done each time the station receives the token whether or not the token is on time.

FDDI relies on the TRT as a priority-adjustment mechanism. In its priority scheme, each station continously monitors TRT, which changes with every byte. A short TRT indicates a lightly loaded network that can accomodate low-priority traffic. During priority allocation, all the stations can accept a set of priority-threshold TRTs. After receiving the token, a station can transmit a data packet only if the TRT is less than the threshold TRT for that packet's priority level.

3.3.6 Applications

There are two major areas of application for FDDI [19]. The first area is backbone applications. FDDI is suitable for this application for at least two reasons. First, its 100 Mbps data rate allows it to support the aggregate bandwidth requirement of several LANs. Second, FDDI can span large distances (up to 2 km) between stations. This allows the backbone network to easily connect multiple buildings in a metropolitan area. An FDDI backbone may connect LANs together through bridges, routers, or gateways, and network planners may utilize FDDI's station management features to analyze network performance (delay, throughput, etc.) and more effectively isolate faults.

The second area of application is the more common and deals with front-end applications. It typically consists of workstations, file servers, and computer servers connected together through concentrators. This provides the advantages of a star topology and improves the reliability of the ring. The FDDI network increases the throughput between the user at the workstation, the file server, and the computer server.

Initial uses of FDDI networks will be evolutionary rather than revolutionary. FDDI can be used as a back-end (I/O channel) interface, a front-end high-performance network, and a backbone network for LAN interconnection. Different features of FDDI make it attractive for these and other applications.

The first FDDI network in the United States was installed in November 1991 by Centel for government users in Tallahassee, Florida [20, 21]. As a result of this MAN, network interconnection services are now available city-wide for more than 20 subscriber networks. More FDDI networks are now being used in many places and the number of installations is growing. However, they are more expensive than lower-speed LANs because FDDI has yet to benefit from production-level pricing. Many expect this per-node differential cost to drop. At that point, FDDI will offer a clear bandwidth/cost advantage over Ethernet and token ring. It is possible to extend the data rate up to 1 Gbps.

3.3.7 FDDI-II

Although FDDI was initially envisioned as a data-only LAN, the full integration of isochro-nous and bursty data traffic is obtained with the enhanced version of the protocol, known as FDDI-II. FDDI-II builds on original FDDI capabilities and supports integrated voice, video, and data capabilities. FDDI-II therefore expands the range of applications of FDDI. FDDI-II can connect high-performance workstations, processors and mass storage systems with bridges, routers, and gateways to other LANs, MANs, and WANs. The evolution of FDDI-II applications will parallel that of the basic FDDI.

Figure 3.13 shows FDDI-II architecture. At the MAC layer, FDDI-II is almost completely the same as for the original FDDI except that two components, the hybrid multiplexer (HMUX) and the isochronous MAC (IMAC), are added. There are no differences at the PHY and PMD layers.

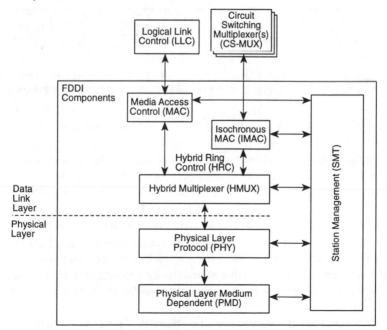

Figure 3.13 FDDI-II architecture.

FDDI-II adds a circuit-switching capability and introduces a frame, whose structure is shown in Figure 3.14. The FDDI- II protocol allows

the stations on the ring to communicate by means of both circuit switching and packet switching. Circuit switching is achieved by means of a
cycle format created by a station known as the *cycle master*. The cycle
master is responsible for creating the cycles at a rate of 8 kHz (every 125
μs, as required for digital PCM speech sampling) and inserts the latency
required to maintain an integral number of cycles synchronously on the
ring. The cycles are repeated by all other stations on the ring. As each
cycle completes its circuit of the ring, it is stripped by the cycle master.

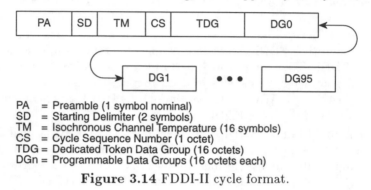

PA = Preamble (1 symbol nominal)
SD = Starting Delimiter (2 symbols)
TM = Isochronous Channel Temperature (16 symbols)
CS = Cycle Sequence Number (1 octet)
TDG = Dedicated Token Data Group (16 octets)
DGn = Programmable Data Groups (16 octets each)

Figure 3.14 FDDI-II cycle format.

The format of the cycles is shown in Figure 3.14. It contains synchronization preamble PA, a start delimiter SD, a TM field indicating
the allocation of the wide-band channels (WBCs, 1 WBC = 6.144 Mbps)
to isochronous or bursty traffic, a cycle sequence (CS) field to correlate
subsequent frames, the TDG field dedicated to data transmissions, and
96 DGn fields comprising of 16 bytes each, the ith byte belonging to the
ith WBC.

FDDI-II supports both packet-switched (synchronous and asynchronous) and circuit-switched (isochronous) traffic. Asynchronous packet traffic occurs in random quantities at random times, whereas synchronous packet traffic occurs regularly in relatively predictable quantities. Circuit-switched traffic is usually isochronous data, which occurs in a precise amounts on a precise time basis. Networks that carry
isochronous data must maintain precise synchronism.

FDDI-II operates in either basic or hybrid mode. An FDDI-II network usually starts out in basic mode, then switches to hybrid mode.
The basic mode of operation is the same as the original FDDI. In this
mode, only the packet-switched service, regulated by the token, is allowed. In the hybrid mode, which is the FDDI-II mode of operation,
both packet and circuit services are allowed. The hybrid mode operation requires the existence of a hybrid ring control (HMUX and IMAC)
entity between the MAC and the PHY. It differs from the basic mode operation in that both FDDI token ring operation and isochromous data
transfer are multiplexed onto the same medium with ring bandwidth

being dynamically allocated between packet and isochronous traffic in units of 6.144 Mbps [22].

Four priority levels are maintained in an FDDI-II network. Isochronous traffic has the highest priority. Second priority is given to synchronous packet traffic. Third priority is given to asynchronous traffic operating in restricted token mode. The lowest priority is assigned to asynchronous traffic that is transmitted only by capturing a nonrestricted token.

3.3.8 FFOL

Just as FDDI is the follow-on LAN for ethernet and token ring LANs, FFOL is the FDDI follow-on LAN. Work on FFOL began in February 1990 by Task Group X3T9.5. The requirements for this next generation FDDI include [23, 24]:

- Ability to provide sufficient bandwidth to act as a backbone for multiple FDDI networks
- Support of all FDDI and FDDI-II data applications (services) and integrated services
- Ability to provide efficient interconnections to WANs
- Duplex links to ensure reliability
- Initial data rate of from 600 Mbps to 1.25 Gbps
- A data rate aligned with synchronous digital hierarchy (SDH)
- Ability to take advantage of existing FDDI cable plant
- Supported physical topologies to include ring and tree topologies so that existing FDDI cable plant may be used
- Provision for appropriate fault isolation, reporting, and recovery mechanisms relatively insensitive to network size and network bit rate
- Provision for mechanisms for reservations, preallocations, and priorities to allow different classes and priorities of services
- Ability to operate over leased public network links
- Support for both single- and multiple- mode fiber
- Media accessing modes for both isochronous and asynchronous services
- Provision for an efficient mechanism for supporting multicast addressing
- Interfaces to standard management entities

A major goal of FFOL is to provide a network service for both data and multimedia applications, and also for traffic emanating from future WANs (e.g., B-ISDN and SMDS). FFOL will require standards to accomplish its goals and requirements. A proposed architecture for FFOL is shown in Figure 3.15.

Standardization efforts on FDDI-II and FFOL are still going on. With the widespread use of the basic FDDI, a broad market for FDDI-

II and FFOL will come. There is also a rapid progress in making FDDI available over copper wires, which are cheaper than optical fibers. This effort is leading to *copper distributed data interface* (CDDI). Attempts are being made to provide broadband video and voice networks to residential customers using a unique combination of fiber, coaxial, and copper technologies [25].

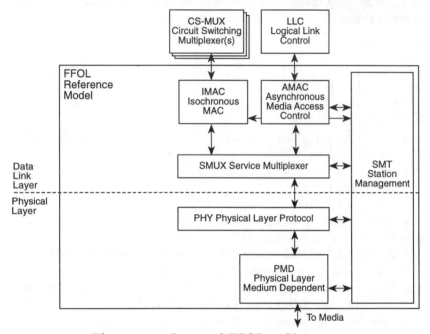

Figure 3.15 Proposed FFOL architecture.

For a complete formal description of FDDI, the reader is referred to the ANSI standard documentation [26]. The history of FDDI is reviewed in [27]. A simplified description of the protocol provided by McCool [28]. Overviews of the concepts and characteristics of FDDI and FDDI-II are provided by Ross [11, 12]. Other issues on the technology, applications, and design of FDDI and FDDI-II are addressed by Mirchandani and Khanna [9] and Kessler and Train [29].

3.4 DQDB

The IEEE 802 committee perceived the need for high-speed services over wide areas and formed the IEEE 802.6 Metropolitan Area Network (MAN) committee in 1982. Several systems were proposed to the IEEE 802.6 committee, but in November 1987 the committee reached a consensus to use Distributed-Queue Dual-Bus (DQDB) as the standard medium-access-control (MAC) protocol. DQDB is modeled after the Queued Packet and Synchronous Exchange (QPSX) protocol, developed at the University of Western Australia and proposed by Telecom Australia to the IEEE 802.6 committee [30–32]. Besides being a MAC standard for MAN, DQDB is also regarded by the ANSI T1S1.1 committee as the major component in the broadband ISDN user network interface standard.

Based on DQDB, vendors can build components that will allow communication services within a metropolitan area exceeding 50 km in diameter.

3.4.1 Basic Features

The DQDB standard is both a protocol and a subnetwork. It is a subnetwork in that it is a component in a collection of networks to provide a service. For example, multiple DQDB subnetworks could be interconnected by bridges, routers, or gateways to form MANs and WANs. The term *distributed-queue, dual-bus* refers to the use of a dual-bus topology and a MAC technique based on the maintenance of distributed queues. In other words, each station connected to the subnetwork maintains queues of outstanding requests that determine access to the MAN medium. The DQDB MAC protocol may be regarded as a hybrid multiplexer managing both circuit-switching and packet-switching traffic.

The DQDB subnetwork has many features, some of which make it attractive for high-speed data services [32]:

- *Shared Media:* It extends the capabilities of shared media systems over large geographical areas.
- *Fault Tolerance:* It is tolerant to transmission faults when the system is configured in a loop.
- *Congestion Control:* It is based on a distributed queuing algorithm as a way of resolving congestion. This protocol ensures that a high utilization of the transmission resources and their fair allocation are possible under overload conditions. Also, a priority mechanism is provided that enables a network operator to provide preferential performance to some types of traffic over other types.
- *Connectionless Service Provision:* It provides a connectionless services at the MAC layer as other IEEE LANs.
- *Segmentation:* Its use of ATM technique allows long, variable-length packets to be segmented into short, fixed-length segments.
- *Flexibility:* It is able to utilize a variety of media, including coaxial cable and fiber optics. It can simultaneously support both circuit-switched and packet-switched services. item• *Compatibility:* It is compatible with current IEEE 802 LANs and future networks such as B-ISDN. In fact, many view DQDB as an early implementation of B-ISDN.

The DQDB standard allows a MAN to be formed by interconnecting DQDB subnetworks via bridges, routers, and gateways. DQDB may also serve as a backbone network. A major difference between DQDB and most of the earlier slotted networks is that a reverse channel is used to reserve slots. Also, DQDB supports traffic of multiple priority levels . The network span of about 50 km, transmission rate of about 150 Mbps, and slot size of 53 bytes allow many slots to be in transit between the nodes.

3.4.2 Architecture

The DQDB dual-bus topology is identical to that used in Fasnet, as shown in Figure 3.4. As both buses are operational at all times, the capacity of the subnetwork is twice the capacity of each bus. In this network, nodes are connected to two unidirectional buses, which operate independently and propagate in opposite directions as shown in Figure 3.16. The nodes are attached to both buses via a logically OR writing tap and a reading tap that is logically placed ahead of the writing tap. Every node is able to send information on one bus and receive on the other bus. The head station (frame generator) generates a frame every 125 μs to suit digitized voice requirement. The frames are continously generated on each bus so that there is never any period of silence on the bus. The frame is subdivided into equal-sized slots. The empty slots generated can be written into by other nodes. The end station (slave frame generator) terminates the forward bus, removes all incoming slots and generates the same slot pattern at the same transmission rate on the opposite bus [33]. (The node at the head of the bus is sometimes the *head of bus* [HOB].) The slots are 53 octets long, the same as ATM cells, to make DQDB MANs compatible with BISDN.

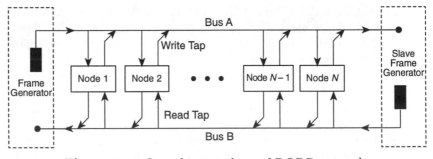

Figure 3.16 Open bus topology of DQDB network.

The subnetwork operates in one of two topologies: open bus (Figure 3.16) or looped bus (Figure 3.17). The two topologies provide basically the same service. The looped bus topology is well suited for network configuration in case of physical break or failure. A single node is the head of both buses in a looped bus topology, whereas two stations take on the HOB functions in open bus architecture.

The functional architecture of a typical DQDB node consists of the physical layer and the DQDB MAC layer, as shown in Figure 3.18. The physical layer, which corresponds with the OSI physical layer, is responsible for timing and synchronization issues and monitoring the error rate on the incoming transmission links to ensure quality service. The layer incorporates a convergence protocol, which provides a consistent service to the DQDB layer regardless of the transmission system. The three transmission systems referenced in the standard are DS3 transmitting at 44.736 Mbps over coaxial cable or fiber, SONET transmitting at 155.2 Mbps over single-mode fiber, and G.703, which transmits at 34.368 Mbps and 139.264 Mpbs over a metallic medium.

The DQDB layer is equivalent to the MAC sublayer. It is responsible for addressing, framing, sequencing, error detection, medium access control, fragmenting messages into individual slots, and reassembling slots into messages. It is intended to provide three major services:

1. A connectionless data service, which provides support for connectionless MAC data service to LLC

2. An isochronous service, which provides support for users who require a constant interarrival time. This allows the transfer of data between two isochronous service users over an already established isochronous connection.

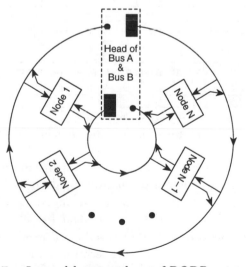

Figure 3.17   Looped bus topology of DQDB network.

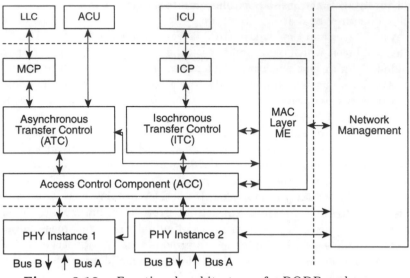

Figure 3.18   Functional architecture of a DQDB node.

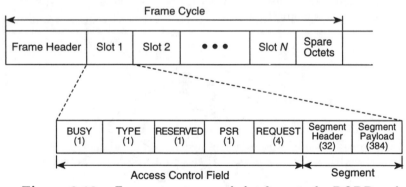

Figure 3.19   Frame structure and slot format of a DQDB node.

3. A connection-oriented data service, which supports the transfer of
   segments between nodes sharing a virtual channel connection

3.4.3 Frame Structure

In a DQDB subnetwork, the frame (and consequently the transmission
bandwidth) is segmented in slots. The frame structure and slot format
are shown in Figure 3.19. Each slot consists of a 53-byte transmission
unit for isochronous and asynchronous traffic, comprised of a 1-byte access control field (ACF), a 4-byte segment header, and a 48-byte segment
payload.

The ACF (the first byte of each segment header) is composed of 8 bits (1 octet or 1 byte) whose functions are as follows:

1. BUSY: This bit indicates if the slot has data (BUSY = 1), or can be accessed (BUSY = 0).

2. TYPE: There are two slot types, and this bit indicates whether the slot is *prearbitrated* (PA) for transfering isochronous segments, TYPE = 1 or is *queue arbitrated* (QA) for carrying asynchronous segments, TYPE = 0. The prearbitrated access mode is reserved for isochronous services, that is, services that require a fixed but smooth bandwidth, such as voice and video services.

3. RESERVED: This bit is for future use and is presently set to 0.

4. PSR: This indicates whether or not the previous slot has been received.

5. REQUEST: There are four REQUEST bits indicating if a slot contains a request for transmissions. The four bits offer four priority levels.

A segment consists of a header and a payload as shown in Figure 3.20. The segment payload carries the 48 bytes of data. In PA segments, the segments may be shared by a number of isochronous service users. In QA segments, the contents of the payload are not restricted. The segment header field consists of the following:

1. Virtual channel identifier (VCI): This is a 20-bit field used in identifying the virtual channel to which the segment belongs. (A virtual channel is a logical connection.) Since there is no destination or source address associated with an isochronous connection, the VCI and the byte offset determine the byte in a PA slot that has been preassigned to a node. The VCI value of all ones (hexadecimal FFFFF) corresponds to the connectionless service; other nonzero VCI values are for other services.

2. Payload type: A 2-bit field indicating the type of data being transmitted. It is presently set to 00 for user data.

3. Segment Priority: Another 2-bit field presently set to 00 for a multiport bridge, which connects many subnetworks.

4. Header check sequence: This 8-bit field is meant for detecting error in the segment header field. The generating polynomial used for this purpose is

$$G(x) = x^8 + x^2 + x + 1 \tag{3.2}$$

3.4.4 Access Mechanism

Unique to the DQDB subnetwork is the concept of *distributed queues* (DQs). Unlike the local queues, the distributed queues are merely logical and do not represent any physical queues. The service mechanism within each distributed queue is nonpreemptive priority queueing of segments with FCFS for each priority. The distributed queue is implemented by having stations keep track of segment requests from stations down-stream, as observed on the reverse bus. To achieve this, each station has a set of two physical counters per priority: the *request-bit counter* (RBC) and the *countdown counter* (CDC), as shown in Figure 3.21. The RBC keeps track of current empty-slot requirements of the downstream stations, whereas the content of the CDC indicates the number of empty slots to be passed before the station's own data transmission takes place. Access to the buses is controlled by these counters.

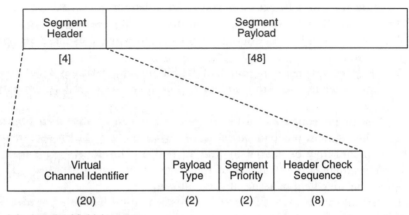
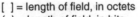
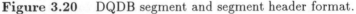

[ ] = length of field, in octets
( ) = length of field, in bits

Figure 3.20   DQDB segment and segment header format.

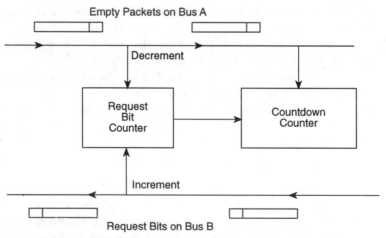

Figure 3.21 The request and countdown counters.

As mentioned earlier, two types of slots are carried on the bus: queued arbitrated (QA) and prearbitrated (PA) slots. Corresponding to the two kinds of slots are two different access methods: QA and PA.

The QA access method supports services that are not time-sensitive, such as asynchronous data transfer. Nodes gain access to QA slots by using the distributed-queue access protocol augmented by two features designed to optimize the protocol: bandwidth balancing and priorities. This access protocol is a distributed reservation scheme. This implies at least three things: (1) time on the medium is divided into slots; (2) a node that has data to transmit must reserve a future slot; (3) the nodes collectively determine the order in which slots are granted.

When a node has a QA segment to transmit, it chooses the bus that leads to the intended destination (forward bus) and then sends on the other bus requests for free slots. Assume, without loss of generality, that a node is transmitting on bus A and making a request for transmission on bus B. (The same discussion holds true for transmission on bus B because the operation of both buses is identical.) The node joins the distributed queue by putting its request on bus B (thereby informing upstream nodes) and waits for its turn. Each node maintains the state of the distributed queue in a *distributed queue state machine* (DQSM), which monitors the transmission procedure through the request counter and the countdown counter. The DQSM can be in either of two states: *idle* or *countdown*. When a station has no segments to transmit, the DQSM is in the idle state. In that state, the RBC is incremented by 1 for every slot with a reserved request (REQUEST = 1) passing by on bus B, and decremented by 1 for every empty slot (BUSY = 0) passing by on bus A. When the queue has segments to transmit, it enters the countdown state. In that state, the content of RBC is copied into CDC and RBC is reset to 0, then the CDC is decremented by 1 for every empty slot passing by on bus A. Through the CDC, each node knows how many empty slots it must let pass by before its turn. When the value of the CDC reaches 0, the station grabs the next empty slot, sets the BUSY bit to 1 and writes its data on the payload field. After the station accesses the slot, it enters the idle state again and monitors the requests as before.

A station is allowed to send only one request for every transmission and cannot send another request before it transmits the segment corresponding to its previous reservation. Only after a request has been serviced can the next request be sent. Hence, for two buses and four priority levels, there can be at most eight pending requests for each station. To summarize, to gain access on a bus using the QA protocol, a node

- Sends a request for transmission to the upstream nodes
- Joins the distributed queue by using the countdown counter
- Maintains the distributed queue with the request counter

- Allows the passage of enough empty slots to satisfy the request of the nodes ahead of it in the distributed queue
- Sends its own data when its turn comes

The PA access method supports time-sensitive applications such as isochronous connection–oriented services. Nodes gain access to the PA slots by following a request-and-assign procedure. A node establishes connection with another node by requesting bandwidth from a call/connection control entity. The HOB is responsible for marking the slots and placing a VCI (virtual channel identifier) in the slot header. The HOB also sends a sufficient number of PA slots to meet the requested bandwidth. Each node examines the VCI in passing slots and maintains a table indicating each VCI value it must access and the position(s) within the slot for reading and/or writing. If the VCI matches one listed in the node's table, the node reads from and/or writes into the appropriate position(s) in the slot.

Unlike in a pure ring architecture, data does not pass through each station. A station on the bus reads the addresses of passing information slots and copies the data if the destination address in the information slot matches that of the station.

DQDB is able to integrate traffic with two different priorities, where the lowest priority is subdivided into four priority levels. The high-priority slots are allocated by the master station to be shared between a number of selected stations; the low-priority slots can be used by all stations.

The major advantages of the network are full bandwidth utilization and low waiting delays. The main cause of performance degradation in DQDB is due to the packet segmentation and the resulting accumulated slot overhead.

3.4.5 Bandwidth Balancing

It has been observed that early versions of DQDB were unable to provide a fair distribution of bandwidth to stations under overload traffic conditions, because upstream stations can use a larger transmission bandwidth than downstream stations, and stations using a larger amount of bandwidth tend to prevent other stations' access. One way of explaining this unfairness issue is that the DQDB protocol pushes the system too hard. The problem was overcome by adding the *bandwidth balancing* (BWB) mechanism to the protocol [34–37]. The main purpose of the modified protocol is to compel heavy users not to take unfair advantage of their position and monopolize the network. The BWB mechanism leaks some bandwidth in order to prevent the hogging of bandwidth under overload conditions. It does this by forcing nodes whose offered load is larger than the available bandwidth to be rate controlled. Each of these nodes is allocated a fraction R of the available bandwidth. The value of R is

$$R = \frac{\beta(1 - S)}{1 + N\beta} \tag{3.3}$$

where S is the total bandwidth used by the nodes that are not rate controlled, N is the number of nodes that are rate controlled, and β is a proportionality constant known as the BWB modulus. With a startup value (or default value) of 8, the value of β varies from 0 to 64 and is set according to traffic conditions.

To implement the BWB mechanism, one more counter for each direction at each node is required. This counter, known as the *trigger counter* (TRC) is increased by 1 every time the node transmits a data segment. When the value of the TRC reaches the value of β, the RBC is increased by 1 and the TRC is set to 0. This artificial increment of the RBC forces the rate-controlled node to let one empty slot pass by on the node after every β slots, even though no request was sent by the downstream nodes. The downstream nodes may not use this empty slot, resulting in bandwidth wastage. Thus, the bandwidth balancing mechanism creates some other problems. It forces the network to leave a certain percentage of the available bandwidth unused, so full bandwidth utilization is given up to provide fairness to all stations. Also, the four levels of priority given by the original protocol are eliminated. Another modification has been proposed to solve the issue of bandwidth unfairness without creating any other problems [38, 39]. Nevertheless, DQDB shows superior performance compared with other protocols considered earlier in this chapter.

Since its adoption by the IEEE 802.6 committee, the DQDB subnetwork has generated a significant interest due to the simplicity of its medium access control protocol. This intense interest has led to a literature explosion on DQDB. A review of literature on DQDB is given by Mukherjee and Bisdikian [40] and an annotated bibliography of related papers on DQDB by Sadiku and Arvind [41]. More details of DQDB are provided by the IEEE 802.6 working group [42].

3.5 Comparison of DQDB and FDDI

One may legitimately ask, "How does DQDB fare in comparison with FDDI?" This question has received a lot of attention and generated a lot of debate. The comparisons made were based on a variety of parameters, and the overall conclusion is that there is no clear winner. Although the two protocols essentially provide similar services, they have different characteristics, which lead to different performances.

DQDB and FDDI share the same advantages and disadvanges with other bus and ring networks. These include the following [2]:

- A bus is generally more reliable than a ring because the station-to-cable connection is passive in a bus.

- A bus causes less propagation delay than a ring because each station connected to the ring may likely examine the address field of a message to decide whether to take of the message or pass it to the next station.
- A bus has a better distributed failure recovery characteristic than a ring.
- A ring can cover longer distances than a bus because each station acts like a repeater.
- It is easier to implement a ring using optical fiber because of its point-to-point connection as opposed to the multiple drop connection required in a bus.
- The access delay is deterministic in a ring, but random in a bus if a contention scheme is used.

Besides the topological differences, other differences can be considered in terms of parameters such as (1) throughput, (2) efficiency, (3) access delay, (4) response time, (5) priority, (6) fairness, (7) reliability, (8) network reconfiguration, and (9) compatibility [43–45].

- *Throughput:* This is the portion of the bandwidth that is usable under heavy load. The maximum throughput or utilization of a network depends on several factors, such as the transmission rate and the overhead. Since DQDB has two buses, each with a rate of 155 Mbps, the network can offer over 300 Mbps bandwidth. FDDI uses two rings, each with a rate of 100 Mbps, but only the primary ring is used for transmission. The other ring serves as backup. Thus, FDDI actually operates effectively at half of its physical limit of 100 Mbps. The bandwidth loss of DQDB and FDDI due to overhead varies. FDDI is more effective for long messages; DQDB is more effective for short ones.
- *Efficiency:* This is the ratio of the total bandwidth utilized to the total available. It is directly related to the network throughput and transmission rate. Figure 3.22 portrays the efficiency of FDDI and DQDB as a function of bus/ring lengths (for 1,000 nodes and TTRT = 1 ms), and Figure 3.23 shows efficiency as a function of number of nodes (for 100 km and TTRT = 5 ms). (TTRT is the target token-rotation time used to control access of FDDI nodes to the ring.) The figures suggest that FDDI is more efficient than DQDB for short distances and a small number of nodes. However, when either the distance or number of nodes is large, DQDB proves to be superior.
- *Access Delay:* This is how long a node has to wait for the opportunity to transmit its message. The maximum delay of a network depends on several parameters such as message length, traffic loading, traffic type, priority scheme, network span, and network size.

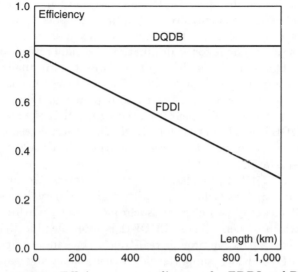

Figure 3.22 Efficiency versus distance for FDDI and DQDB [43].

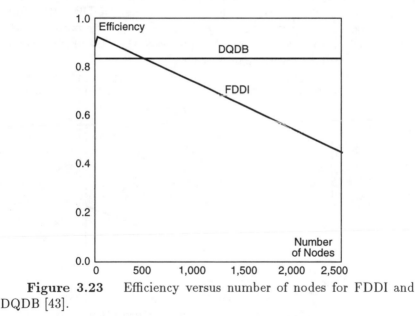

Figure 3.23 Efficiency versus number of nodes for FDDI and DQDB [43].

For asynchronous traffic, FDDI performs better for long messages because of its exhaustive service discipline, whereas DQDB performs better for short messages. DQDB performs better for a network at longer distance or with larger number of nodes, whereas FDDI performs better over a limited area. Thus, FDDI is better suited for communications characterized by long message length and small

communication distance. DQDB, on the other hand, is better suited
for applications that involve sending messages over a wide area.

- *Response Time:* This is the time taken by a short message to go
  from the source node to the destination node and return to its source
  node. This is perhaps the most important performance measure
  from the end user's point of view. The response time as a function
  of distance and number of nodes is depicted in Figures 3.24 and
  3.25, respectively. It is clear from the figures that the response time
  for DQDB is less than that for FDDI. The superior response time of
  DQDB is due to its slot structure and the reduced average distance
  between stations.

- *Priority:* FDDI-II provides three priority classes: isochronous, synchronous, and asynchronous, with eight priority levels, whereas
  DQDB has only two classes: isochronous and asynchronous, with
  four priority levels. Thus, FDDI-II is more flexible than DQDB.
  However, DQDB can provide real-time service more efficiently than
  basic FDDI, which supports only synchronous and asynchronous
  classes.

- *Fairness:* FDDI uses the ring topology, which is a symmetric topology, so FDDI supports fair access to its users. DQDB suffers from
  unfairness due to its asymmetric bus structure. The fairness of the
  DQDB protocol is even more pronounced when the traffic loading
  is high or the network span is large.

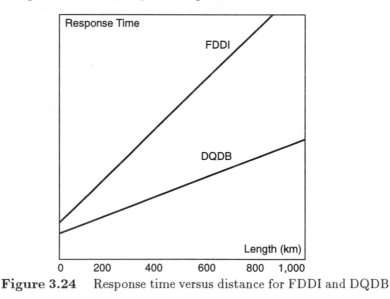

Figure 3.24   Response time versus distance for FDDI and DQDB
[43].

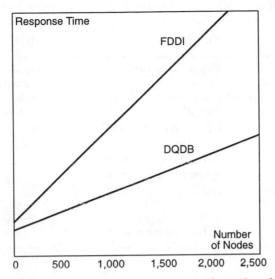

Figure 3.25 Response time versus number of nodes for FDDI and DQDB [43].

- *Realibility:* DQDB employs a very efficient way to bypass failed nodes, whereas FDDI needs to loop the primary ring back to the secondary ring (thereby increasing the round-trip propagation delay) and reinitialize the ring. Also, DQDB is simpler than FDDI and consequently more reliable. The complexity of FDDI decreases the protocol's reliability.

- *Network Reconfiguration:* Again, due to simpler operation, it is easy for DQDB to reconfigure itself without affecting regular operations, whereas FDDI has to reinitialize every time a node is added or deleted, thereby requiring a lot of processing and delay.

- *Compatibility:* Compatibility with present and future networks is important. The DQDB has a physical layer designed to be medium independent to allow for future transmission media and rates. It has excellent compatibility with ATM and therefore has unique characteristics and service definitions, which correspond to those adopted for BISDN. On the other hand, messages in the FDDI network are transmitted in variable-length format. Thus an interface is needed to connect FDDI and ATM networks.

A brief summary of the comparison is given in Table 3.3. Overall, it seems that the performance characteristics of FDDI and DQDB match the interests of the respective forums that created them; FDDI has been created in a mostly computer-industry forum, whereas DQDB has been created in a mostly telecommunications-industry forum.

Table 3.3   Comparison of FDDI and DQDB.

Features	FDDI	DQDB
Topology	Single/dual ring	Dual bus
Medium access	Token	Distributed queue
Physical medium	Fiber optics	Independent
Data rate	100 Mbps	150 Mbps
Traffic type	FDDI: synchronous/ asynchronous FDDI-II: isochronous/ synchronous/asynchronous	Isochronous/ synchronous
Suitability for public network	No	Yes
Status	FDDI available FDDI-II concept	Trial

3.6 Other MANs

Besides the four protocols considered so far in this chapter, several other MAN technologies have been proposed or developed. Some of these are briefly discussed in this section.

3.6.1 Orwell Ring

The Orwell slotted ring MAN is being developed by British Telecom Research Laboratories for optical fiber networks operating at over 100 Mbps [16, 46, 47]. It was modeled after the Cambridge ring LAN, where the ring is partitioned into time slots of equal lengths. It was designed with the following objectives in mind:

1. To increase transmission capacity by freeing slots as soon as they reach their destination rather than waiting to remove them when they return to their source
2. To control requests so as to ensure that the delays for different request types are kept minimum
3. For compatibility with the BISDN. All services are converted to ATM cells for transport via fixed-length slots.

Stations are actively coupled to the ring. They may act as concentrators for requests submitted by more than one node. These requests may of be different types (e.g., data, voice, video) and are assembled into packets, which are then transported to the destination stations by slots. The stations repeat or modify the slots. Slots circulate around the ring and may be full or empty. Each station is capable of using every empty slot that arrives and reading every slot destined to it. A full slot is released by the source station, emptied by the destination station, and passed on by the destination station to the next station on the ring as an empty slot. This is a major departure from other slotted ring protocols, such as the Cambridge ring, where a slot can only be emptied by the source node. This procedure allows the ring to have up to twice the throughput capacity of a ring that is based on source slot control. However, the efficiency of release at destination is accompanied by a potentially unfair sharing of the communication resource.

A mechanism that provides a fair access and prevents hogging is built into the Orwell protocol. Orwell has an efficient access protocol compared to other high-speed rings. Although the Orwell slotted ring MAN appears to offer a viable alternative to DQDB protocol, no attempt has been made to obtain international standardization approval for the former.

3.6.2 MAGNET

MAGNET was designed and implemented at Columbia University in New York as a network testbed for integrated MANs [47–51]. It consists of two counterrotating rings that interconnect a set of stations and operate at a link rate of 100 Mbps. The physical level of MAGNET is configured as a single optical fiber connecting the nodes in tandem. MAGNET uses an 8-bit destination address, thus allowing a maximum of 256 stations.

MAGNET supports three classes of traffic, each with up to four priority levels. The traffic classes represent an abstract performance-oriented concept that can support services such as data, video, voice, graphics, and facsmile. MAGNET may be regarded as a distributed switch that establishes connections between nodes. Switching is based on the principle of asynchronous time sharing (ATS), which refers to the manner in which scheduling resolves contention between the different traffic classes. This allows the three traffic classes to enter any switch fabric sequentially. The main requirement is that the quality of service is guaranteed during the period of a call.

The enhanced version of MAGNET, known as MAGNET II, supports isochronous and asynchronous traffic [51–53]. MAGNET II consists of a set of switching nodes (or stations) that are interconnected via T3 links in loop topology. Each station on the network is connected to both rings. One station acts as the head station, with additional hardware for ring timing and control. Under the normal mode of operation, any of the two rings will provide a connection between any two stations and the traffic is shared by both rings, thus yielding a total link capacity of 200 Mbps. If a ring fails, the network is switched to a single-ring operation mode.

3.6.3 Homenet

Homenet is a broadband system that supports data, real-time digitized voice, and analog video on a single cable in a CATV type of network [54]. It combines frequency and time multiplexing and uses distributed packet switching techniques so that all switching functions are performed at the user's terminal equipment. It overcomes the distance limitation in LANs by dividing the large CATV network into smaller *homenets*. Each homenet (or *net* for short) consists of a large number of users within a small geographical region and is assigned a 6-MHz frequency band. Users transmit their data/voice on a single frequency, which is then translated to its homenet frequency and broadcast in such a manner that all the users in all nets can receive it. The problem of guaranteeing the continuity of a nondistorted speech signal at the receiver is solved using a communication protocol known as *movable slot time division multiplexing* (MSTDM), which is a variation of the CSMA/CD protocol. Collisions are detected by comparing every bit of a packet before and after transmission.

3.7 Conclusion

This chapter has highlighted some of the key features of popular high-speed networks proposed as MANs. Some other high-speed networks proposed as LANs and MANs are discussed in by Li and his colleagues [44] and by Abeysundara and Kamal [55]. The networks differ in the precise way in which they schedule traffic for transmission on the medium.

Although the current Gbps network is regarded as a milestone compared with the existing Mbps networks, it is only a small fraction of the rates possible with fiber-optic technology. Therefore, the study of high-speed networks will continue for many years to come.

References

[1] M. Gerla and L. Fratta, "Tree Structured Fiber Optics MAN's," *IEEE Journal on Selected Areas in Communications,* vol. SAC-6, no. 6, July 1988, pp. 934–943.

[2] C. W. Tseng and B. U. Chen, "D-Net, a New Scheme for High Data Rate Optical Local Area Networks," *IEEE Journal on Selected Areas in Communications,* vol. 81, no. 3, April 1983, pp. 493–499.

[3] F. A. Tobagi, F. Borgonovo, and L. Fratta, "Expressnet: a High-Performance Integrated-service Local Area Network," *IEEE Journal on Selected Areas in Communications,* vol. SAC-1, no. 5, Nov. 1983, pp. 898–913.

[4] F. A. Tobagi and M. Fine, "Performance of Unidirectional Broadcast Local Area Networks: Expressnet and Fasnet," *IEEE Journal on Selected Areas in Communications,* vol. SAC-1, no. 5, Nov. 1983, pp. 913–926.

[5] F. Borgonovo, "ExpressMAN: Exploiting Traffic Locality in Expressnet," *IEEE Journal on Selected Areas in Communications,* vol. SAC-5, no. 9, Dec. 1987, pp. 1436–1443.

[6] J. O. Limb, "Fasnet: Proposal for a High Speed Local Network," in N. Naffah (ed.), *Office Information Systems.* Amsterdam: North-Holland, 1982, pp. 87–91.

[7] J. O. Limb and C. Flores, "Description of Fasnet — A Unidirectional Local-Area Communication Network," *Bell System Technical Journal,* vol. 61, no. 7, Sept. 1982, pp. 1413–1440. Also in B. G. Kim (ed.), *Current Advances in LANs, MANs, and ISDN.* Norwood, MA: Artech House, 1989, pp. 185–212.

[8] J. O. Limb and L. E. Flamm, "A Distributed Local Area Network Packet Protocol for Combined Voice and Data Transmission," *IEEE Journal on Selected Areas in Communications,* vol. SAC-1, no. 5, Nov. 1983, pp. 926–934.

[9] S. Mirchandani and R. Khanna (eds.), *FDDI: Technology and Applications.* New York: John Wiley & Sons, 1993.

[10] W. E. Burr, "The FDDI Data Optical Link," *IEEE Communications Magazine,* vol. 24, no. 5, May 1986, pp. 8–23.

[11] F. E. Ross, "FDDI —A Tutorial," *IEEE Communications Magazine,* vol. 24, no. 5, May 1986, pp. 10–17.

[12] F. E. Ross, "An Overview of FDDI: The Fiber Distributed Data Interface," *IEEE Journal on Selected Areas in Communications,* vol. SAC-7, no. 7, Sept. 1989, pp. 1043–1051. Also in C. Dhas *et al.* (eds), *Broadband Switching: Architectures, Protocols, Design, and Analysis.* Los Alamitos, CA: IEEE Computer Society Press, 1991, pp. 50–58.

[13] D. Tsao, "FDDI: Chapter Two," *Data Communications,* Dec. 21, 1991, pp. 59–70.

[14] S. P. Joshi, "High-Performance Networks: A Focus on the Fiber Distributed Data Interface (FDDI) Standard," *IEEE Micro,* vol. 6, no. 3, June 1986, pp. 8–14.

[15] G. Watson and D. Cunningham, "FDDI and Beyond: A Network for the 90s," *IEEE Review,* April 1990, pp. 131–134.

[16] J. Houldsworth *et al., Open System LANs and Their Global Interconnection.* Oxford: Butterworth-Heinemann, 1991, pp. 3.85–3.103, 10.13–10.32.

[17] S. P. Joshi and V. Iyer, "FDDI's 100 Mbps Protocol Improves on 802.5 Spec's 4 Mbps Limit," *EDN,* May 2, 1985, pp. 151–156, 158, 160.

[18] F. E. Ross and J. R. Hamstra, "FDDI — A LAN Among MANs," *Computer Communication Review,* vol. 20, no. 3, July 1990, pp. 16–31.

[19] K. Parker, "An Introduction to FDDI Technology, Applications and Markets," *Conference Record of Wescon/90*, Nov. 1990, pp. 102–104.

[20] W. M. Price and J. F. Westmark, "Tallahassee's CMDS: The First FDDI MAN," *Business Communications Review*, vol. 21, no. 10, 1991, pp. 37–41.

[21] W. M. Price, "MAN Provides FDDI to Tallahassee," *Telephony*, Feb. 1993, pp. 16–17.

[22] M. Teener, "AN FDDI/FDDI-II Interoperation Strategy," *Conference Record of Wes-con/90*, Nov. 1990, pp. 114–117.

[23] R. L. Fink and F. Ross, "FFOL — an FDDI Follow-On LAN," *Computer Communication Review*, vol. 21, no. 2, April 1991, pp. 15–16.

[24] F. E. Ross and R. L. Fink, "Overview of FFOL —FDDI Follow-On LAN," *Computer Communications*, vol. 15, no. 1, Jan./Feb. 1992, pp. 5–10.

[25] R. Karpinski, "US West Forges Ahead with Fiber/Coax Vision," *Telephony*, Feb. 8, 1993, pp. 7–8.

[26] "FDDI Token Ring Media Access Control," ANSI Standard X3T9.5, 1988.

[27] F. E. Ross and J. R. Hamstra, "Forging FDDI," *IEEE Journal of Selected Areas in Communications*, vol. 11, no. 2, Feb. 1993, pp. 181–190.

[28] J. F. McCool, "FDDI: Getting to Know the Inside of the Ring," *Data Communication Magazine*, vol. 17, no. 3, March 1988, pp. 185–192.

[29] G. C. Kessler and D. A. Train, *Metropolitan Area Networks*. New York: McGraw-Hill, 1992.

[30] J. F. Mollenauer, "Standards Metropolitan Area Networks," *IEEE Communication Magazine*, vol. 26, no. 4, April 1988, pp. 15–19.

[31] R. M. Newman, Z. L. Budrikis, and J. L. Hullett, "The QPSX Man," *IEEE Communications Magazine*, vol. 26, no. 4, April 1988, pp. 20–28. Also in C. Dhas *et al.* (eds), *Broadband Switching: Architectures, Protocols, Design, and Analysis.* Los Alamitos, CA: IEEE Computer Society Press, 1991, pp. 59–67.

[32] M. Littlewood, "Metropolitan Area Networks and Broadband ISDN: A Perspective," *Telecommunication Journal of Australia*, vol. 39, no. 2, 1989, pp. 37–44.

[33] K. Sauer and W. Schodl, "Performance Aspects of the DQDB Protocol," *Computer Networks and ISDN Systems*, vol. 20, 1990, pp. 253–260.

[34] M. Zuckerman and P. G. Potter, "The DQDB Protocol and its Performance under Overload Traffic Conditions," *Computer Networks and ISDN Systems*, vol. 20, 1990, pp. 261–270.

[35] V. P. T. Phung and R. Breault, "On the Unpredictable Behavior of DQDB," *Computer Networks and ISDN Systems,* vol. 24, 1992, pp. 145–152.

[36] C. C. Bisdikian, "A Performance Analysis of the IEEE 802.6 (DQDB) Subnetwork with the Bandwidth Balancing Mechanism," *Computer Networks and ISDN Systems,* vol. 24, 1992, pp. 367–385.

[37] W. Stallings, *Networking Standards.* Reading, MA: Addison-Wesley, 1993, pp. 398- -433.

[38] Z. Liu *et al.,* "Performance Analysis of DQDB Metropolitan Subnetwork," *Proceedings of IEEE Southeast Conference,* 1993.

[39] G. G. Patramanis, "Performance Analysis of Metropolitan Area Subnetwork," M. Sc. Thesis, Department of Electrical Engr., Temple University, Philadelphia, January, 1993.

[40] B. Mukherjee and C. Bisdikian, "A Journey Through the DQDB Network Literature," *Performance Evaluation,* vol. 165, December 1992, pp. 129–158.

[41] M. N. O. Sadiku and A. S. Arvind, "An Annotated Bibliography of Distributed Queue Dual Bus (DQDB)," *Computer Communication Review,* vol. 24, no. 1, January 1994, pp. 21–36.

[42] IEEE 802.6 Working Group, "Proposed IEEE Standard 802.6 — Distributed Queue Dual Bus (DQDB) —Metropolitan Area Network (MAN)," Draft versions: June 1988, Nov. 1988, Spring 1989, August 1989.

[43] M. A. Rodrigues, "Evaluating Performance of High-speed Multiaccess Networks," *IEEE Network Magazine,* vol. 4, no. 2, May 1990, pp. 36–41.

[44] V. O. K. Li *et al.,* "A Survey of Research and Standards in High-Speed Networks," *International Journal of Digital and Analog Communication Systems,* vol. 4, no. 4, 1991, pp. 269–309.

[45] F. Tari and V. S. Frost, "Performance Comparison of DQDB and FDDI for Integrated Networks," *Proceedings of 16th IEEE Conference on Local Computer Networks,* 1991, pp. 96 105.

[46] R. M. Falconer and L. Adams, "Orwell: A Protocol for an Integrated Services Local Network," *British Telecommunication Technical Journal,* vol. 3, no. 4, October 1985, pp. 27–28.

[47] I. Mitrani *et al.,* "A Modelling Study of the Orwell Protocol," in O. J. Boxma, J. W. Cohen, and H. C. Tijms (eds.), *Teletraffic Analysis and Computer Performance Evaluation.* Amsterdam: North-Holland, 1986, pp. 429–438.

[48] A. A. Lazar *et al.,* "MAGNET: Columbia's Integrated Network Testbed," *IEEE Journal on Selected Areas in Communications,* vol. SAC-3, no. 6, Nov. 1985, pp. 859–871.

[49] A. Patir *et al.,* "An Optical Fiber-based Integrated LAN for MAGNET's Testbed Environment," *IEEE Journal on Selected Areas in Communications,* vol. SAC-3, no. 6, Nov. 1985, pp. 872- -881.

[50] A. A. Lazar and J. S. White, "Packetized Video on MAGNET," *Optical Engineering*, vol. 26, no. 7, July 1987, pp. 596–602.

[51] M. El Zarki *et al.*, "Performance Evaluation of MAGNET Protocols," in R. L. Pickholtz (ed.), *Local Area and Multiple Access Networks*. Rockville, MD: Computer Science Press, 1986, pp. 137–154.

[52] A. A. Lazar, G. Pacifici, and J. S. White, "Real-Time Traffic Measurements on MAGNET II," *IEEE Journal on Selected Areas in Communications*, vol. 8, no. 3, April 1990, pp. 467–483.

[53] A. A. Lazar, A. T. Temple, and R. Gidron, "MAGNET II: A Metropolitan Area Network Based on Asynchronous Time Sharing," *IEEE Journal on Selected Areas in Communications*, vol. 8, no. 8, Oct. 1990, pp. 1582–1594.

[54] M. Hatamian and E. G. Bowen, "Homenet: A Broadband Voice/Data/Video Network on CATV Systems," *AT & T Technical Journal*, vol. 64, no. 2, Feb. 1985, pp. 347–367.

[55] B. W. Abeysundara and A. E. Kamal, "High-Speed Local Area Networks and Their Performance: A Survey," *ACM Computing Surveys*, vol. 23, no. 2, June 1991, pp. 221–264.

Chapter 4

Performance Analysis

Shallow men believe in luck, strong men in cause and effect.
—Ralph Waldo Emerson

Modeling and performance analysis play an important role in the design of communication systems. Models are tools for designers to study a system before it is actually implemented. Performance evaluation of models of computer networks during the architecture design, development, and implementation stages provides means to assess critical issues and components. It enables one to select the best design strategy from the alternative solutions. It also gives the designer the freedom and flexibility to adjust various parameters of the network in the planning rather than the operational phase.

The purpose of this chapter is to obtain the performance analysis of common MAN topologies. Sections 4.1 to 4.3 deal with the analysis of interconnected token rings via a backbone ring, DQDB subnetwork, and FDDI ring respectively. The modeling and performance analysis of each of these networks is extremely difficult because it is hard to describe the interactions among a plethora of processes that make up the network. For this reason, only an approximate analysis of each system is given.

A major performance criterion is the mean transfer delay of a message, which is defined as the time from the instant a message becomes available for transmission at a station until the end of its successful reception at the destination. Delay results are useful for designing communication systems. Other performance criteria used include throughput efficiency and fairness.

4.1 Interconnected Token Rings

A fundamental problem one faces in analyzing interconnected systems is that of characterizing the departure process of the successfully transmitted messages. Describing the process is a difficult task. Therefore, the complexity of the interconnected systems defies exact mathematically tractable solutions. Notwithstanding this, several attempts [1–15] have been made to analyze the performance of interconnected LANs because of the importance of such networks. Such attempts, based on special assumptions, have been carried out through simulation, measurement, approximate analytical solutions, or a combination of these. Only the approximate analysis of interconnected token rings by Ibe and Cheng [2, 3] is presented here.

In the interconnected token ring network system, the individual LANs are connected to a backbone ring via a bridge. The backbone ring is a high-speed fiber distributed data interface (FDDI), as portrayed in Figure 4.1. Each bridge performs a routing and flow control function and is modeled as two independent stations, as shown in Figure 4.2; one station receives a packet from the backbone ring and transmits it into the local ring, whereas the other station receives from the local ring and transmits into the backbone ring. The packets are buffered in the bridge until they are successfully transmitted into the appropriate ring.

There are two kinds of messages (internetwork and intranetwork) and two modes of operation (priority and nonpriority) in an interconnected token ring network system. In the nonpriority mode, the bridge

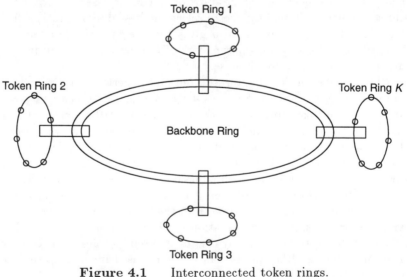

Figure 4.1   Interconnected token rings.

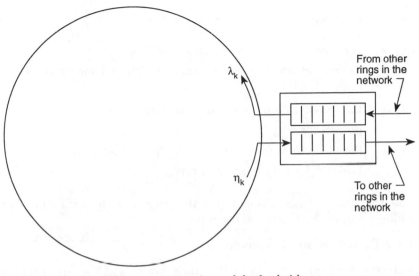

Figure 4.2   A model of a bridge.

and all other stations can transmit at most one message each time they receive the token. In the priority mode, on the other hand, the bridge transmits exhaustively but other stations can transmit at most one message upon receiving the token. It is assumed that the network operates in the priority mode in this chapter.

We consider a system with K token rings network labeled $1, \ldots, K$ connected to a FDDI backbone ring as shown in Figure 4.1. In each token ring there are $N_k - 1$ identical stations and a bridge.

4.1.1 Notation

It is appropriate to define the following terms to be used in the analysis.

$B_{jk} =$ the time required to transmit a frame at station j of ring k (i.e., the service time); b_{jk} and $b_{jk}^{(2)}$ are its first and second moments

$C_k =$ the mean cycle time in ring k

$L_k =$ the length of each message and is assumed to have general distribution for ring k

$q_{kl} =$ the probability that a message generated in ring k is destined for ring l

$R_{jk} =$ the switchover time from station $j - 1$ to station j in ring k; r_{jk} and $r_{jk}^{(2)}$ are its first and second moments

$s_k =$ the total mean walk time in ring k; i.e., $s_k = \sum_{l=1}^{N_k} r_{kl}$

$w_{jk} =$ the mean waiting time at node j of ring k

$\eta_k =$ the rate at which messages arrive at bridge k for transmission in the backbone ring

$\lambda_k =$ the arrival rate of messages that form a Poisson process for ring k

$\Lambda_k =$ the rate at which messages arrive from other rings at bridge k for transmission in ring k

Note that the switchover time is variably known as the walk time, the polling time, or the token-passing time.

4.1.2 Distribution of Arrivals

A stream of messages arrive at each station on ring k at the same average rate of λ_k, which is an independent Poisson process. The number of stations sending messages to bridge k from its own ring has a binomial distribution with parameters $N_k - 1$ and $q = 1 - q_{kk}$. Therefore, the probability of n stations sending messages to the bridge is [1]

$$P(n) = \begin{bmatrix} N_k - 1 \\ n \end{bmatrix} q^n (1 - q)^{N_k - 1 - n}. \tag{4.1}$$

Since the stations that communicate with each other are most likely on the same ring, the probability q of a station sending messages to stations on other rings is usually small. Also, the number of stations $N_k - 1$ is often large (more than 20). For small q and large N_k, this binomial distribution approximates a Poisson distribution. Thus, the arrival process to the bridge can be approximated to be Poisson with parameter $(N_k - 1)(1 - q_{kk})$. In an average cycle time C_k, an average of $(N_k - 1)(1 - q_{kk})$ messages arrive at bridge k so the arrival rate at the bridge is

$$\eta_k = (N_k - 1)\lambda_k(1 - q_{kk}), k = 1, \ldots, K \tag{4.2}$$

As we have shown, the arrival of messages to the bridge is Poisson. Because the sum of independent Poisson processes is also Poisson, the arrival process of messages from other rings is Poisson distributed with rate

$$\Lambda_k = \sum_{l=1, l \neq k}^{K} (N_k - 1)\lambda_k q_{kl}, \ k = 1, \ldots, K \tag{4.3}$$

4.1.3 Calculation of Delays

Delay is measured as the transfer time of the packets and defined as the time interval from generation of a packet at the source station to its reception at the destination. This means that the transfer time includes the queuing time (or waiting delay) at the source station, the source bridge delay, and destination bridge delay. The mean transfer delay of a message is therefore the sum of the following terms:

D_{ss}^k = the mean message delay at the source station

τ_s^k = the propagation delay from the source station to the source bridge

D_{sb}^k = the mean delay at the source bridge

τ_{sd}^{kl} = the propagation delay between the source bridge and the destination bridge

D_{db}^l = the mean delay at the destination bridge

τ_d^l = the propagation delay between the destination bridge and the destination station

Thus, the total mean delay is defined by

$$D_{total}^k = D_{ss}^k + D_{sb}^k + D_{db}^l + \tau_s^k + \tau_{sd}^{kl} + \tau_d^l \tag{4.4}$$

In general the propagation delays are negligibly small compared to other delays and can be ignored. Therefore, the total mean delay in Eq. (4.4) becomes

$$D_{total}^{kl} = D_{ss}^k + D_{sb}^k + D_{db}^l \tag{4.5}$$

For the local message, the mean message delivery time for the message in ring k is

$$D_{local}^k = D_{ss}^k \tag{4.6}$$

For an arbitrary message generated in ring k, the mean message delivery time is given by

$$D_{arb}^k = q_{kk} D_{ss}^k + \sum_{k \neq l} q_{kl} D_{total}^{kl} \tag{4.7}$$

Arbitrary delay denotes the delay of a message that is generated in a ring but has an arbitrary destination, which could be the ring itself or any other ring. Substituting Eq. (4.5) into Eq. (4.7) gives

$$D_{arb}^k = q_{kk} D_{ss}^k + \sum_{k \neq l} q_{kl} (D_{ss}^k + D_{sb}^k + D_{db}^l)$$

where

$$q_{kk} + \sum_{k \neq l} q_{kl} = 1$$

Thus,

$$D_{arb}^k = D_{ss}^k + \sum_{k \neq l} q_{kl}(D_{sb}^k + D_{db}^l) \tag{4.8}$$

Following Ibe and Cheng's mathematical model [2], it is assumed that all the stations in each ring are labeled $2, \ldots, N_k$, whereas a bridge is labeled as node 1. Since it is assumed that all the stations are identical in each ring, the local delay and the delay at the destination bridge are given by

$$D_{ss}^k = w_{2k} + b_{2k} \tag{4.9}$$

$$D_{db}^k = w_{1k} + b_{1k} \tag{4.10}$$

where node 2 represents any nonbridge station; w_{1k} and w_{2k} are the waiting delays at the destination bridge and source station, respectively; and b_{1k} and b_{2k} are the respective service times. The traffic intensities at the bridge and each station in ring k are respectively given by

$$\rho_{1k} = \Lambda_k b_{1k} = \sum_{l=1, l \neq k}^{K} (N_k - 1)\lambda_k q_{kl} b_{1k} \tag{4.11}$$

and

$$\rho_{2k} = \lambda_k b_{2k} \tag{4.12}$$

The total traffic intensity of the ring k is the sum of the two traffic intensities and is given by

$$\rho_k = \rho_{1k} + (N_k - 1)\rho_{2k} \tag{4.13}$$

The mean cycle time is defined as the mean time between two successive visits of the server to a particular node and is given by

$$C_k = \frac{s_k}{1 - \rho_k} \tag{4.14}$$

where

$$s_k = \sum_{k=1}^{N_k} r_k \tag{4.15}$$

In terms of these variables, the mean waiting time at the destination bridge is given by [2, 3]:

$$w_{1k} = \frac{\Lambda_k b_{1k}^{(2)}}{2(1 - \rho_{1k})} + \frac{(N_k - 1)\lambda_k b_{2k}^{(2)}}{2(1 - \rho_k + \rho_{2k})}$$

$$+ \frac{(1 - \rho_k)r_{1k}^{(2)} + (N_k - 1)(1 - \rho_{1k} + \rho_{2k})r_{2k}^{(2)}}{2s_k(1 - \rho_{1k})}$$

$$+ \frac{(N_k - 1)\rho_{2k}s_k}{2(1 - \rho_{1k})} + \frac{(N_k - 1)(N_k - 2)\rho_{2k}^2 s_k}{2(1 - \rho_{1k})(1 - \rho_k + \rho_{2k})}$$

$$+ \frac{(N_k - 1)(1 - \rho_k)r_{1k}r_{2k}}{s_k(1 - \rho_{1k})}$$

$$+ \frac{(N_k - 1)\big[(N_k - 2)(1 - \rho_k) - N_k \rho_{2k}\big]r_{2k}^2}{2s_k(1 - \rho_{1k})} \qquad (4.16)$$

The mean waiting time at any nonbridge node in ring k is [2]

$$w_{2k} = \frac{A - 2(1 - \rho_k)\rho_{1k}w_{1k}}{2(N_k - 1)\rho_{2k}(1 - \rho_k - \lambda_k s_k)} \qquad (4.17)$$

where

$$A = \rho_k \big[\Lambda_k b_{1k}^{(2)} + (N_k - 1)\lambda_k b_{2k}^{(2)}\big] + \rho_k(1 - \rho_k)\frac{s_k^{(2)}}{s_k}$$

$$+ s_k \big[\rho_k^2 - \rho_{1k}^2 + (N_k - 1)\rho_{2k}^2\big] \qquad (4.18)$$

To compute the mean delay D_{sb}^k at the source bridge, let X_k denote the mean transmission time of a message in the backbone ring at bridge k, where x_k and $x_k^{(2)}$ are the first and second moments of X_k, respectively. Let

$$\gamma_k = \eta_k x_k \qquad (4.19a)$$

denote the offered load at bridge k, where η_k is the arrival rate at each bridge in the backbone ring. The total traffic intensity γ of the backbone ring is given by

$$\gamma = \sum_{k=1}^{K} \gamma_k \qquad (4.19b)$$

The approximate mean waiting time of the backbone ring at bridge k is given by Everitt [16]

$$w_{sb}^k = \frac{1 - \gamma_k}{2(1 - \gamma)}\left[s_b + \frac{\gamma\Big((1 - \gamma)\Delta_b^2 + s_b \sum\limits_{l=1}^{K} \eta_l x_l^{(2)}\Big)}{s_b \sum\limits_{l=1}^{K} \gamma_l(1 - \gamma_l)}\right] \qquad (4.20)$$

where s_b and Δ_b^2 are respectively the mean and variance of the switchover time of the backbone ring.

The delay at the source bridge is given by

$$D_{sb}^k = w_{sb}^k + x_k \tag{4.21}$$

where x_k is the service time of the backbone ring.

Now the three mean message delivery times given in Eqs. (4.5), (4.6), and (4.8) can be written as

$$D_{local}^k = w_{2k} + b_{2k} \tag{4.22}$$

$$D_{total}^{kl} = D_{local}^k + w_{sb}^k + x_k + w_{1l} + b_{1l} \tag{4.23}$$

$$D_{arb}^k = D_{local}^k + \sum_{k \neq l} q_{kl}(w_{sb}^k + x_k + w_{1l} + b_{1l}) \tag{4.24}$$

where w_{1l} and b_{1l} are the waiting delay and service time at the destination bridge, respectively.

4.1.4 Numerical Examples

Consider an interconnected token ring network for which $N_k = 21$ (i.e., 20 stations and 1 bridge) and $K = 4$ rings with $\lambda_2 = 2\lambda_1$, $\lambda_3 = 3\lambda_1$, and $\lambda_4 = 3\lambda_1$—i.e., asymmetric traffic conditions. The transmission rates for a local ring and the backbone ring are assumed to be 10 and 100 Mbps, respectively. It is assumed that the packet length is 6400 bits, token length is 24 bits, and walk time is $0.005 \times b$ for local ring and $0.0005 \times b$ for backbone ring. This implies that $b_k = 6.4 \times 10^{-4}$ s and $x_k = 6.4 \times 10^{-5}$ s for all k. Throughout the analysis, constant packet length is assumed and all delays are normalized with respect to service time $b \, (= b_k)$.

The assumed routing probabilities q_{kl} are given in Table 4.1. The arrival rates η_k and Λ_k presented in Table 4.2 are calculated using Eqs. (4.2) and (4.3). The traffic intensities ρ_k shown in Table 4.3 are calculated using Eqs. (4.11) to (4.13) and (4.19a).

We use both the analytical model discussed in this section and the simulation model by Murad [17] for the interconnected token ring. For the simulation results, the confidence interval is calculated from

$$X = \overline{Y} \pm \frac{S_Y t_{\alpha/2; N-1}}{\sqrt{N}} \tag{4.25}$$

where $t_{\alpha/2; N-1}$ is the percentage point of the student-t distribution with $N-1$ degrees of freedom, Y_i is the sample value, $N \, (= 5$ for our case) is the number of simulation runs, and S_Y is the sample standard deviation.

The results are presented in terms of delay versus traffic intensity of ring 1 (i.e., ρ_1). Tables 4.4 to 4.6 show a comparison (for ring 2) between analytic and simulation results for local, total (or end-to-end), and arbitrary delays. It is evident from these tables that analytical results agree fairly well with the simulation results.

Figure 4.3 shows the variation of the normalized mean total delay (D_{total}/b) with traffic intensity for constant packet length. It is evident from the figure that in general the mean delay increases with traffic intensity. This should be expected because as the traffic intensity increases many messages are serviced, thereby compelling the arriving message to wait longer.

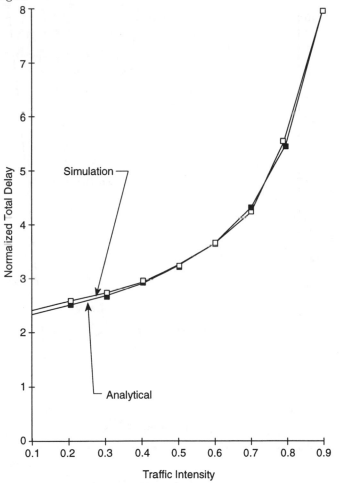

Figure 4.3   Normalized total delay D_{total} versus traffic intensity ρ_1 for ring 2.

Figure 4.4 shows local delay, bridge delay, and backbone delay for
ring 3. It is clear from this figure that the backbone delay is very small
compared to the bridge and local delays. The reasons for this include
the following: (1) the backbone ring operates at a very high speed, (2) it
has very few stations, and (3) it employs an exhaustive service discipline,
which always has less delays. Figure 4.4 also shows that the bridge and
the local delay are almost the same at low traffic intensity. The priority
given to the bridge has no effect on the local and bridge delays at low
to moderate traffic intensities. However, at high traffic intensities it
is observed that the priority for the messages at the bridge makes the
bridge delay much lower than the local delay.

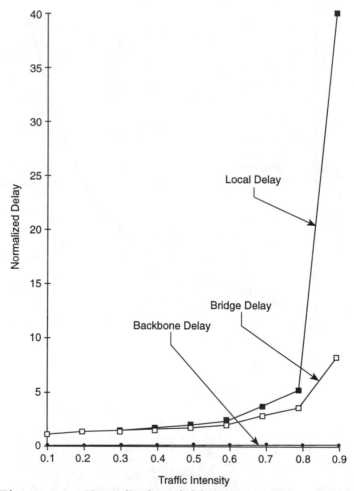

Figure 4.4   Normalized total delays D_{total}, D_{db}, and D_{ab} versus
traffic intensity ρ_1 for ring 3.

Figure 4.5 shows the arbitrary delay for the four rings. These figures show the effect of symmetric traffic conditions (i.e., different arrival rates in each ring) and routing probabilities given in Table 4.1. The arrival rates of rings 1, 2, 3, and 4 are λ_1, $2\lambda_1$, $3\lambda_1$, and $3\lambda_1$, respectively. The arbitrary delay for ring 1 is the lowest because it has the lowest routing probability (i.e., $q_{kl} = 0.1$) for the intermessages. The routing probability for intermessages of rings 2, 3, and 4 are 0.4, 0.6, and 0.5, respectively. Since the routing probabilities are so close for rings 2, 3, and 4, the arrival rates have the dominating effect on the arbitrary delay. This figure shows that the higher the arrival rate of the ring the greater the delay.

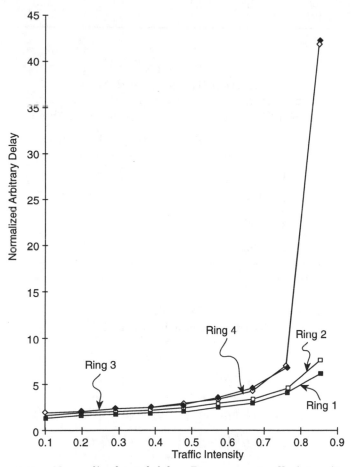

Figure 4.5   Normalized total delay D_{arb} versus traffic intensity ρ_1 for the four rings.

Table 4.1
Routing Probabilities q_{kl}.

		Destination		
Source	1	2	3	4
1	0.9	0.1	0.0	0.0
2	0.2	0.6	0.1	0.1
3	0.3	0.2	0.4	0.1
4	0.3	0.1	0.1	0.5

Table 4.2
Arrival Rates η_k **and** Λ_k.

Arrival from Local Ring to Backbone Ring	Arrival from Backbone Ring to Local Ring
$\eta_1 = 2\lambda_1$	$\Lambda_1 = 44\lambda_1$
$\eta_2 = 16\lambda_1$	$\Lambda_2 = 20\lambda_1$
$\eta_3 = 36\lambda_1$	$\Lambda_3 = 10\lambda_1$
$\eta_4 = 30\lambda_1$	$\Lambda_4 = 10\lambda_1$

Table 4.3
Traffic Intensities ρ_k **and** γ_k.

Traffic Intesity for Local Ring	Traffic Intensity for Backbone Ring
$\rho_1 = 64\lambda_1 b_1$	$\gamma_1 = (0.2/64)\rho_1$
$\rho_2 = (60/64)\rho_1$	$\gamma_1 = (1.6/64)\rho_1$
$\rho_3 = (70/64)\rho_1$	$\gamma_1 = (3.6/64)\rho_1$
$\rho_4 = (70/64)\rho_1$	$\gamma_1 = (3.0/64)\rho_1$

Table 4.4
Normalized Arbitrary Delay D_{arb} for Ring 2.

Traffic Intensity ρ_1	Analytical	Simulation	% Difference
0.1	1.6	1.65 ± 0.01	−3.12
0.2	1.7	1.73 ± 0.011	−2.33
0.3	1.83	1.85 ± 0.023	−1.05
0.4	2.01	1.99 ± 0.027	0.84
0.5	2.24	2.21 ± 0.021	1.18
0.6	2.59	2.52 ± 0.053	2.70
0.7	3.15	3.008 ± 0.085	4.51
0.8	4.2	4.026 ± 0.15	4.14
0.9	7.15	6.576 ± 0.43	8.03

Table 4.5
Normalized Total D_{total} for Ring 2.

Traffic Intensity ρ_1	Analytical	Simulation	% Difference
0.1	2.32	2.38 ± 0.011	−2.93
0.2	2.46	2.52 ± 0.03	−2.76
0.3	2.64	2.68 ± 0.015	−1.74
0.4	2.86	2.88 ± 0.055	−0.98
0.5	3.16	3.17 ± 0.031	−0.32
0.6	3.59	3.59 ± 0.092	−0.06
0.7	4.23	4.17 ± 0.11	1.42
0.8	5.36	5.44 ± 0.1	−1.53
0.9	7.93	7.93 ± 0.43	0.00

Table 4.6
Normalized Local Delay D_{local} for Ring 2

Traffic Intensity ρ_1	Analytical	Simulation	% Difference
0.1	1.11	1.15 ± 0.007	−3.96
0.2	1.19	1.2 ± 0.015	−1.34
0.3	1.28	1.28 ± 0.016	−0.08
0.4	1.41	1.37 ± 0.02	2.84
0.5	1.58	1.51 ± 0.1	4.43
0.6	1.84	1.69 ± 0.069	7.72
0.7	2.24	2.07 ± 0.1	7.32
0.8	2.97	2.72 ± 0.11	8.43
0.9	4.64	4.25 ± 0.46	8.62

4.2 DQDB

Section 3.4 covered the basic features of the distributed-queue dual-bus (DQDB) subnetwork. Here, we consider the two major performance issues facing DQDB: unfairness problem and message delay.

Several analytical models have been used to resolve the issue of unfairness and calculate the mean delay of messages of the DQDB network. Each of these approaches made some simplifying assumptions in order to obtain analytically tractable solutions. Although most of these models do not take many network parameters into considerations, the models provide some useful insight into the performance of the DQDB network. A brief summary of these models is found in [18].

4.2.1 Unfairness Problem

The major advantages of DQDB are the simplicity of its access mechanism and the fact that it can utilize all the channel capacity on either bus independent of the network size and the channel data rate. The DQDB asynchronous service performs quite well under light loads. However, it has been observed that early versions of DQDB were unable to provide a fair distribution of bandwidth to stations under overload traffic conditions, because upstream stations can use a larger transmission bandwidth than downstream stations, and stations using a larger amount of bandwidth tend to prevent the access of other stations. This station-location dependency of the medium access time has been interpreted as an unfairness property of the DQDB protocol.

To overcome this unfairness problem, the idea of adding a *bandwidth balancing* (BWB) mechanism to the original protocol was proposed [19]. This modified protocol has been further developed and analyzed [20–24]. The main purpose of the modified protocol is to compel heavy users not to take unfair advantage of their position and monopolize the network. The BWB mechanism guarantees equal allocations of bus bandwidth to nodes with traffic of the lowest priority level.

The bandwidth balancing technique is implemented by forcing nodes whose offered load is larger than the available bandwidth to be rate controlled. Each of these nodes is allocated a fraction γ of the available bandwidth. The value of γ is the throughput of each of the N rate-controlled nodes and is given by [21]

$$\gamma = \frac{\beta(1-S)}{1+N\beta} \tag{4.26}$$

where S is the total bandwidth used by the nodes that are not rate controlled and β is a proportionality constant known as the BWB modulus. With a startup value (or default value) of 8, the value of β varies from 0 to 64 and is set dynamically according to traffic conditions. The total bus utilization is

$$\rho = S + N\gamma = \frac{S+N\beta}{1+N\beta} \tag{4.27a}$$

The wasted bandwidth is given by

$$W = 1 - \rho = \frac{1-S}{1+N\beta} \tag{4.27b}$$

From (4.26) to (4.27), two things are evident:

1. The maximum network utilization is achieved when all nodes are rate-controlled (in which case $S = 0$ and N is equal to the total number M of active nodes). Thus

$$\rho_{\max} = \frac{N\beta}{1+N\beta} \tag{4.28}$$

2. The worst case occurs when only one node is active and the corresponding wasted bandwidth is $1/(1+\beta)$.

Thus, by forcing each rate-controlled node to acquire no more than a certain fraction of the remaining bandwidth, we make the DQDB protocol converge to a fair operating point. How rapidly this fair operating point is reached depends on how much bandwidth we are willing to sacrifice. The larger the wasted bandwidth, the faster the convergence.

To put this in concrete terms, suppose there are four active nodes ($M = 4$) with average offered loads of $0.15, 0.20, 0.36$, and 0.40 segments per slot time. Only the last two nodes are rate controlled (i.e., $N = 2$)

because their offered loads are more than 0.25. If $\beta = 10$, then $S = 0.15 + 0.20 = 0.35$, $\gamma = 0.31$, and $\rho = 0.97$, so the carried loads are 0.15, 0.20, 0.31, and 0.31, and the wasted bandwidth is 0.03. Based on Eq.(4.29), Figure 4.6 shows the variation of the maximum utilization with the number of active nodes and the BWB modulus β.

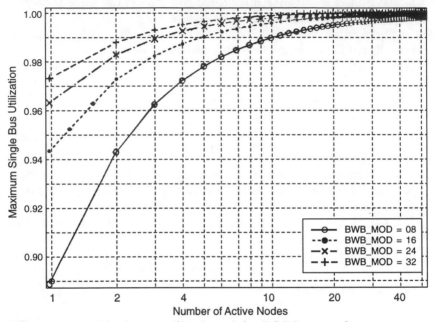

Figure 4.6　　Maximum utilization of the DQDB network versus num-ber of active nodes.

Though this bandwidth balancing mechanism is simple and inge-nious, it creates some other problems. It forces the network to leave a certain percentage of the available bandwidth unused; thus full band-width utilization is lost at the expense of fairness to all stations. Also, the four levels of priority by the original protocol are eliminated. In view of this, several modifications have been proposed [25–39].

4.2.2 Delay Analysis

The overwhelming majority of studies on message delay on DQDB have been based on simulations. Only few analytical models [40–50] have been attempted because of the complexity of the various processes that describe the operation of the network. Only one of the models is dis-cussed here. Other models are discussed by Mukherjee and Bisdikian [18], Bisdikian [42], and Jing and Paterakis [43].

The single-buffer DQDB model assumes that each node has a buffer size of ℓ, where ℓ is the fixed message length in packets. Assume also that time is slotted and that the slot boundaries coincide with those of the slots in the forward channel of the network. The model carries out the performance of the network with respect to a tagged node. It partitions the network into a L-Net (for the left portion of the network), the tagged node, and a R-Net (for the right portion of the network), as shown in Figure 4.7. This way, all nodes to the left and right of the tagged network are aggregated together in the L-Net and R-Net, respectively. With no interest whatsoever on the identity of the originating node, the tagged node sees the L-Net as a generator of busy slots on bus A and the R-Net as a generator of requests on bus B, respectively.

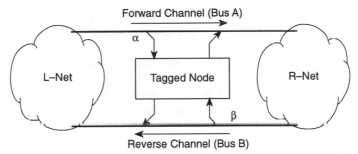

Figure 4.7 The tagged node with its L-Net and R-Net [6].

Let α and β represent the rates at which the L-Net and R-Net respectively transmit packets. In other words, the tagged node senses a busy slot on bus A with probability α and a slot with a request on bus B with probability β. Also let the arrival time be exponentially distributed with parameter λ. Assuming that the time interval between the transmission of a packet and the generation of the next one is geometrically distributed, an imbedded Markov chain is formulated describing the number of requests registered by the tagged node at the instant of a packet arrival. From the Markov chain, the sojourn time (waiting time plus transmission time) of the packet is determined. If D denotes the sojourn time, its mean value is given by [43]

$$E(D) = \frac{E(F)}{1-\alpha}\frac{1-\rho^\ell}{1-\rho} + \frac{\ell}{(1-\alpha)(1-\rho)} - \frac{\rho(1-\rho^\ell)}{(1-\alpha)(1-\rho)^2} \qquad (4.29a)$$

where

$$E(F) = \frac{\rho}{1-\rho} + \frac{e^{-\lambda}}{(1-e^{-\lambda})(1-\rho^\ell)} \cdot [\alpha\beta - (1-\alpha)(1-\beta)(1-\phi_o)] \qquad (4.29b)$$

$$\rho = \frac{\beta}{1-\alpha} \qquad (4.29c)$$

and ϕ_o is the probability that a packet experiences no waiting time. The value of ϕ_o is determined numerically from the analysis of the Markov chain. However, the value of $E(D)$ can be obtained for the lower bound of $\phi_o = 0$ and the upper bound of $\phi_o = 1$. It should be observed that with large value of ℓ in Eq. (4.29a), the quantity $\frac{\ell}{(1-\alpha)(1-\rho)}$ becomes dominant—i.e., for sufficiently large messages, the message delay varies linearly with the message size. We must bear in mind that Eq. (4.29) is based on the fact that the system is in steady state whenever the probability $1 - \alpha$ that the forward channel slot is empty is greater than the probability β that the reverse channel slot contains a request:

$$1 - \alpha > \beta$$

or

$$\alpha + \beta < 1 \tag{4.30}$$

Thus, in order to maintain system stability, an increase in α dictates a corresponding decrease in β. As a result, a single node in the L-Net can shut down the entire R-Net. This confirms the position-dependent characteristic of DQDB, which causes unfairness among the nodes or users.

4.3 FDDI

In Section 3.3, a brief overview of FDDI was given. More features of FDDI are given here to help understand the performance analysis of the network.

FDDI allows two major kinds of traffic: synchronous traffic, which is highly time sensitive, such as voice and video, and asynchronous traffic, which is not time critical, such as data. In order to support the two types of traffic, a timed- token protocol is used in FDDI. For this reason, FDDI MAC protocol is often called the *timed-token protocol.* This protocol guarantees real-time delivery for synchronous traffic while providing prompt delivery for asynchronous traffic.

During the network initialization process, all stations connected to the ring negotiate a target token-rotation time (TTRT) to ensure that each station's requirements could be met. Each station is assigned a portion of the TTRT for the transmission of its synchronous packets, and the remaining bandwidth is used for asynchronous traffic. The value of TTRT is made small enough to satisfy the real-time constraints of synchronous traffic. Each station keeps track of the time when it was last visited by a token. Synchronous traffic may be transmitted unconditionally upon token capture. Asynchronous traffic, however, is controlled by the token-rotation time (TRT), which is the time interval between two successive arrivals of a token at a station. If TRT < TTRT when the token arrives, the value of TRT is copied into the token holding timer (THT), which begins to count upward. Asynchronous frames may now be transmitted until THT reaches the value of TTRT. On the other hand, if TRT > TTRT, the token arrives late and only synchronous traffic may be served. In case different asynchronous priorities are implemented, each priority level j will have its own threshold TRT Pri(j) $\leq$ TTRT, $j = 1, \ldots, 8$.

The timed-token protocol has two important properties [51–53]:
- The average value of TRT is at most TTRT.
- The maximum TRT is at most twice TTRT.

(FDDI can support synchronous traffic only because TRT is bounded.) This implies that during the negotiation process for TTRT, each station should request a value of half the required TRT to support its synchronous traffic. Since the traffic on the network is random, TRT may sometimes exceed TTRT but will never go beyond twice TTRT. This deterministic feature of the protocol makes FDDI an attractive alternative for real-time transmission.

In this section, we evaluate the performance of FDDI ring according to the following criteria [54]: (1) throughput efficiency, (2) delay, and (3) fairness.

4.3.1 Notation

The following terms will be used in the analysis:

C_{ij} = the jth token-rotation cycle, measured between successive arrivals of the token at station i, where the cycle index j is incremented when the token arrives at station j

L = the cable length

N = the number of stations

R = the transmission rate

T = the target token-rotation time (TTRT)

T_{ij}^s = the transmission time of the synchronous traffic at station i during cycle C_{ij}

T_{ij}^a = the transmission time of the asynchronous traffic at station i during cycle C_{ij}

S = the station latency

u = the propagation speed = 200 km/ms or 2×10^8 m/s

γ = the throughput

ρ = the utilization or offered traffic load

τ = the total ring latency

4.3.2 Throughput Analysis

Let α_i be the fraction of the TTRT of station i allocated for synchronous traffic. Then $\alpha_i T$ is the maximum time that can be spent initiating synchronous frame transmission at station i. The total synchronous bandwidth allocation is

$$\alpha = \sum_{i}^{N} \alpha_i \tag{4.31}$$

The total ring latency τ is determined by the number of stations N, the propagation speed u, the cable length L, and the station latency S. It includes the propagation delay time for a complete circuit of the ring and latencies in all stations; that is,

$$\tau = \frac{L}{u} + NS \qquad (4.32)$$

Under steady-state conditions, the utilization is related to the throughput γ and the transmission rate R according to

$$\rho = \frac{\gamma}{R}$$

The maximum utilization that can be achieved when a single asynchronous traffic class is used is

$$\rho_{\max} = \frac{\gamma_{\max}}{R} \qquad (4.33)$$

When α is small enough to allow asynchronous transmission (i.e. $\alpha < 1 - \tau/T$) then $N + 1$ cycles have a total length of $NT + \alpha T + \tau$ during which synchronous traffic is transmitted for $(N + 1)\alpha T$ time units and asynchronous traffic is transmitted for $N(T - \alpha T - \tau)$ time units. Thus, for the symmetric traffic case and $\alpha < 1 - \tau/T$, the maximum synchronous, asynchronous, and total utilizations are given respectively as [54]

$$\rho^s_{\max} = \frac{(N+1)\alpha T}{NT + \alpha T + \tau} \qquad (4.34a)$$

$$\rho^a_{\max} = \frac{N(T - \alpha T - \tau)}{NT + \alpha T + \tau} \qquad (4.34b)$$

$$\rho_{\max} = \rho^s_{\max} + \rho^a_{\max} = \frac{N(T - \tau) + \alpha T}{NT + \alpha T + \tau} \qquad (4.34c)$$

Notice from Eq. (4.34c) that α increases with the maximum utilization. This implies that the maximum utilization is smallest when only asynchronous traffic is present. Also, note that for the case of pure asynchronous traffic (i.e., $\alpha = 0$), Eq. (4.34) becomes

$$\rho^a_{\max} = \frac{N(T - \tau)}{NT + \tau} \qquad (4.35)$$

Combining Eqs. (4.32) and (4.35) gives

$$\rho^a_{\max} = \frac{N\left(T - \dfrac{L}{u} - NS\right)}{NT + \dfrac{L}{u} + NS} \qquad (4.36)$$

This shows the effects of the key system parameters on ρ_{max}. Typical results based on Eq. (4.36) are shown in Table 4.7. The results show that for ring sizes of less than 50 km, FDDI can support utilizations of 0.9 or greater for TTRT values that are 5 ms or greater [54].

Table 4.7
Maximum utilization ρ_{max} for $N = 500$ and $S = 0.5\ \mu s$ [54].

			T	
L	1 ms	2 ms	5 ms	10 ms
1 km	0.745	0.872	0.949	0.975
10 km	0.700	0.850	0.940	0.970
20 km	0.650	0.825	0.930	0.965
50 km	0.500	0.750	0.900	0.950
100 km	0.250	0.650	0.850	0.925

4.3.3 Delay Analysis

The delay analysis of FDDI is a difficult problem. None of the well known service disciplines (limited, gated, or exhaustive) are appropriate for modeling an FDDI MAC protocol. Although the stations are served exhaustively, this exhaustive service may be interrupted by the token holding timer (THT). Also, the time of the THT is not fixed but dynamically controlled by the last token rotation. In spite of this complexity, however, several attempts have been made to provide approximate solutions [48, 49, 54–62]. We follow the one in Lu and Liu [55], which assumes a polling model with exhaustive service discipline, shown in Figure 4.8.

To make the analysis tractable, we make the following assumptions:

1. There are N stations connected to the FDDI ring, and they are uniformly distributed over the ring.
2. The arrival process for synchronous traffic at station i is Poisson with arrival rate λ_i^s.
3. Asynchronous traffic at station i has only one priority level, and the arrival process at the station is Poisson with arrival rate λ_i^a.
4. The frame length for synchronous traffic at station i has a general distribution with mean β_i^s and second moment $\beta_i^{s(2)}$.
5. The frame length for asynchronous traffic at station i has a general distribution with mean β_i^a and second moment $\beta_i^{a(2)}$.

6. The switchover time from station i to station $(i + 1)$ has a general distribution with mean s_i and second moment $s_i^{(2)}$.

7. All stations are symmetric. If ρ_i^s and ρ_i^a denote the offered loads for synchronous and asynchronous traffic at station i, then

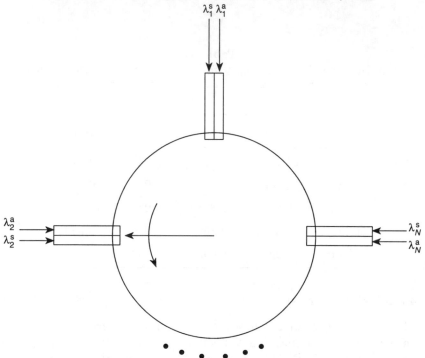

Figure 4.8   A polling model for FDDI ring.

$$\rho_i^s = \lambda_i^s \beta_i^s \qquad (4.37a)$$

$$\rho_i^a = \lambda_i^a \beta_i^a \qquad (4.37b)$$

The total offered load ρ on the ring is

$$\rho = \sum_{i=1}^{N} \rho_i^s + \sum_{i=1}^{N} \rho_i^a = \rho^s + \rho^a \qquad (4.38)$$

The mean waiting times for the synchronous and asynchronous traffic are respectively given by [55]

$$E[W^s] = \frac{(1 - \rho^s)A_e}{\left(\rho - N[(\rho^s)^2 + (\rho^a)^2]\right)} \qquad (4.39)$$

$$E[W^a] = \frac{(1 - \rho^a)A_e}{\left(\rho - N[(\rho^s)^2 + (\rho^a)^2]\right)} \qquad (4.40)$$

where

$$A_e = \rho \frac{N\left[\lambda^s \beta^{s(2)} + \lambda^a \beta^{a(2)}\right]}{2(1-\rho)} + \rho \frac{s^{(2)}}{2s}$$
$$+ \frac{s}{2(1-\rho)} \left(\rho^2 - N[(\rho^s)^2 + (\rho^a)^2]\right) \qquad (4.41)$$

s and $s^{(2)}$ are the mean and second moment of the total switchover time.

Using Eqs.(4.39) to (4.41), the mean waiting times are calculated for the following parameters:

Number of stations $N = 20$.

Transmission rate $R = 100$ Mbps.

$N\rho_i^a = 0.4$ (i.e., total offered load is $\rho = 0.4 + N\rho_i^s$)

Constant synchronous frame length $= 1,040$ bytes, or $\beta^s = 83.2\,\mu$s.

Constant asynchronous frame length $= 4,040$ bytes, or $\beta^a = 323.2\,\mu$s.

Total ring latency $\tau = 15\,\mu$s.

Target token rotation time $T = 100\,\mu$s.

Constant switchover time $s_i = 30$ m for all stations.

Figures 4.9 and 4.10 respectively show the mean waiting time for synchronous and asynchronous frames as the total offered load varies from 0.45 to 0.95 (as the synchronous traffic $N\rho_i^s$ varies from 5% to 55%). Compared with the simulation results [55], the percentage error of the analytical solution in Eqs.(4.39) to (4.41) is less than 6%, confirming the validity of the model. The model also confirms the observation that the FDDI protocol behaves like an exhaustive service system for low offered load but deviates significantly at high loads. That is, at low loads the token holding timer (THT) of FDDI rarely expires, so each station is served exhaustively [54].

4.3.4 Fairness Analysis

The fairness characteristic of FDDI is one of its major strengths. This is now briefly demonstrated for asynchronous traffic ($\alpha = 0$). For a full-queues situation and a constant ring latency [54],

$$T_{ij}^a = T - C_{i,j-1} \qquad (4.42)$$

or

$$T_{ij}^a + \sum_{k=1}^{N} T_{k,j-1}^a + \sum_{k=1}^{i-1} T_{kj}^a = T - \tau \qquad (4.43)$$

By taking the mean of each term and rearranging terms, we obtain

$$\bar{T}_i^a = T - \tau - \sum_{k=1}^{N} \bar{T}_k^a \qquad \text{for all } i \qquad (4.44)$$

where $\bar{T}_i^a$ denotes the mean of T_{ij}^a. We conclude from Eq.(4.44) that $\bar{T}_i^a$ is the same for all i because the right-hand side of the equation is independent of i. Equation (4.44) becomes

$$\bar{T}_i^a = \frac{T - \tau}{N + 1} \quad \text{for all } i \tag{4.45}$$

We notice that each station gets the same amount of bandwidth under full load. Thus, the FDDI protocol is a fair mechanism for controlling access to the ring.

4.4 Conclusion

This chapter has presented the performance evaluation of three common topologies of the metropolitan area networks, namely, the interconnected token rings, DQDB, and FDDI. The performance analysis of interconnected token bus or CSMA/CD networks is very difficult, but some attempts have been made in analyzing such networks [8–11, 17, 63–65].

The closed-form solutions presented in the chapter are representative of the preliminary attempts. It is expected that more work will be done to fine tune the solutions. However, it is hoped that the solutions presented in the chapter will provide network designers with an insight into the performance of the respective systems.

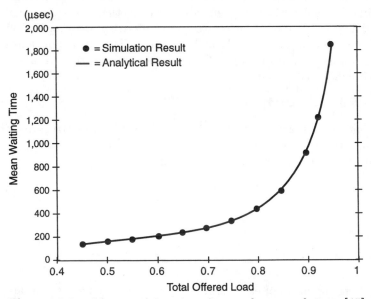

Figure 4.9   Mean waiting time for synchronous frames [45].

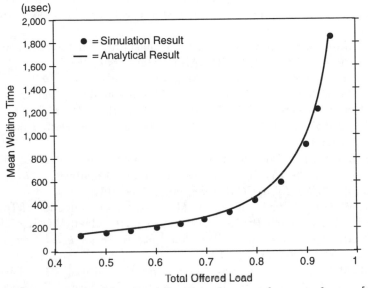

Figure 4.10   Mean waiting time for asynchronous frames [45].

References

[1] R. Kuruppillai and N. Bengtson, "Performance Analysis in Local Area Networks of Interconnected Token Rings," *Computer Communications*, vol. 11, no. 2, April 1988, pp. 59–64.

[2] O. C. Ibe and X. Cheng, "Analysis of Interconnected Systems of Token Ring Networks," *Computer Communications*, vol. 13, no. 3, 1990, pp. 136- -142.

[3] O. C. Ibe and X. Cheng, "Approximate Analysis of Asymmetric Single-Service Token-Passing Systems," *IEEE Transactions on Communications*, vol. 37, no. 6, June 1989, pp. 572–577.

[4] W. Bux and D. Gillo, "Flow Control in Local Area Networks of Interconnected Token Rings," *IEEE Transactions on Communications*, vol. 33, no. 10, October 1985, pp. 1058–1066.

[5] I. Rubin and J. K. Lee, "Performance Analysis of Interconnected Metropolitan Area Circuit-Switched Telecommunications Networks," *IEEE Transactions on Communications*, vol. 36, no. 2, Feb. 1988, pp.171–185.

[6] I. Stavrakakis and D. Kazakos, "Performance Analysis of a Star Topology of Interconnected Networks Under 2nd-Order Markov Network Output Processes," *IEEE Transactions on Communications*, vol. 38, no. 10, Oct. 1990, pp. 1724–1731.

[7] B. Berg and R. H. Deng, "End-to-end Performance of Interconnected LANs," *Computer Communications*, vol. 14, no. 2, March 1991, pp. 105–112.

[8] G. S. Poo, "Performance Measurement of Interconnected CSMA/ CD LANs," *Computer Communications*, vol. 12, no. 1, Feb. 1989, pp. 3–9.

[9] T. Kaneko, S. Hosokawa, and K. Yamashita, "An Interconnection Method of Two CSMA/CD LANs," *Memoirs of the Faculty of Engineering, Osaka City University*, vol. 29, 1988, pp. 81–89.

[10] G. M. Exley and L. F. Merakos, "Throughput-Delay Performance of Interconnected CSMA Local Area Networks," *IEEE Journal on Selected Areas in Communications*, vol. 5, no. 9, Dec. 1987, pp. 1380–1390.

[11] J. L. C. Wu, J. Wu, and T. C. Lee, "Performance Analysis of Interconnected CSMA/CD Networks with Finite Population," *Proceedings of IEEE INFOCOM*, 1988, pp. 1005–1011.

[12] T. M. Tsai, C. Bisdikian, and L. Merakos, "Interconnection of Token Ring LANs Using Bridges: An Approximate Mean Waiting Time Analysis," *Proceedings of the 13th Conference on Local Computer Networks*, 1988, pp. 72–81.

[13] M. Mehmet-Ali, B. Grela-M'Poko, and J. F. Hayes, "The Performance of Interconnected Ring Networks with Priority," *Proceedings of IEEE GLOBECOM*,, 1988, pp. 1803–1807.

[14] X. Meng, R. E. Kinicki, and T. A. Gonsalves, "Delay Analysis of a Metropolitan Area Network," *Proceedings of IEEE 9th Annual International Phoenix Conference on Computers and Communications*, 1990, pp. 568–574.

[15] M. Murata and H. Takagi, "Performance of Token Ring Networks with a Finite Capacity Bridge," *Computer Networks and ISDN Systems*, vol. 24, 1992, pp. 45–64.

[16] D. Everitt, "Simple Approximation for Token Rings," *IEEE Transactions on Communications*, vol. 34, no. 7, July 1986, pp. 719–721.

[17] S. Murad, "Performance Analysis of Interconnected LANs," M. Sc. Thesis, Department of Electrical Engr., Temple University, Philadelphia, May 1993.

[18] B. Mukherjee and C. Bisdikian, "A Journey Through the DQDB Network Literature," *Performance Evaluation*, vol. 165, December 1992, pp. 129–158.

[19] E. L. Hahne, A. K. Choudhury, and N. F. Maxemchuk, "Improving the Fairness of DQDB Networks," *Proceedings of IEEE INFOCOM*, 1990, pp. 175–184.

[20] E. L. Hahne and N. F. Maxemchuk, "Fair Access of Multi-Priority Traffic to Distributed-Queue Dual-Bus Networks," *Proceedings of IEEE INFOCOM*, 1991, pp. 889–900.

[21] E. L. Hahne, A. K. Choudhury, and N. F. Maxemchuk, "DQDB Networks with and Without Bandwidth Balancing," *IEEE Transactions on Communications,* vol. 40, no. 7, July 1992, pp. 1192–1204.

[22] M. Zuckerman and P. G. Potter, "The DQDB Protocol and Its Performance Under Overload Traffic Conditions," *Computer Networks and ISDN Systems,* vol. 20, 1990, pp. 261–270.

[23] V. P. T. Phung and R. Breault, "On the Unpredictable Behavior of DQDB," *Computer Networks and ISDN Systems,* vol. 24, 1992, pp. 145–152.

[24] C. Bisdikian, "A Performance Analysis of the IEEE 802.6 (DQDB) Subnetwork with the Bandwidth Balancing Mechanism," *Computer Networks and ISDN Systems,* vol. 24, 1992, pp. 367 385.

[25] B. Mukherjee and S. Banerjee, "Alternative Strategies for Improving the Fairness in and an Analytical Model of DQDB Networks," *Proceedings of IEEE INFOCOM,* 1991, pp. 879–888.

[26] M. Conti, E. Gregori, and L. Lenzini, "DQDB/FBS: a Fair MAC Protocol Stemming from DQDB Fairness Analysis," *Proceedings of the 2nd IEEE Workshop on Future Trends of Distributed Computing Systems,* 1900, pp. 66–74.

[27] K. M. Khalil and M. E. Koblentz, "A Comparative Performance Analysis of Distributed Queue Dual Bus Access Control Methods," *Proceedings of the 2nd IEEE Workshop on Future Trends of Distributed Computing Systems,* 1900, pp. 75–79.

[28] E. Y. Huang and L. F. Merakos, "On the Access Fairness of the DQDB MAN Protocol," *Proceedings of the IEEE 9th Annual International Phoenix Conference on Computers and Communications,* 1990, pp. 556–559.

[29] M. A. Rodrigues, "Erasure Node: Performance Improvements for the IEEE 802.6 MAN," *Proceedings of IEEE INFOCOM,* 1990, pp. 636–643.

[30] I. J. Hyun and K. J. Han, "Dynamic Bandwidth Balancing Mechanism for Improving DQDB Performance," *Proceedings of IEEE ICC,* 1991, pp. 1345–1349.

[31] Z. Liu *et al.,* "Performance Analysis of DQDB Metropolitan Subnetwork," *Proceedings of IEEE Southeast Conference,* 1993.

[32] G. G. Patramanis, "Performance Analysis of Metropolitan Area Subnetwork," M. Sc. Thesis, Department of Electrical Engr., Temple University, Philadelphia, January, 1993.

[33] F. Borgonovo *et al.,* "FQDB: A Fair Multisegment MAC Protocol for Dual Bus Networks," *IEEE Journal on Selected Areas in Communications,* vol. 11, no. 8, Oct. 1993, pp. 1240–1248.

[34] ——, "Performance of FQDB, a Fair MAC Protocol for Dual Bus Networks," *Proceedings of IEEE INFOCOM,* 1992, pp. 210–218.

[35] Y. Gong and M. Paterakis, "Design and Performance Analysis of a Dynamic Protocol Achieving User Fairness in High-Speed Dual-Bus Networks," *Proceedings of IEEE INFOCOM*, 1992, pp. 1079–1088.

[36] S. Y. Cheung, "Controlled Request DQDB: Achieving Fairness and Maximum Throughput in the DQDB Network," *Proceedings of IEEE INFOCOM*, 1992, pp. 180–189.

[37] L. N. Kumar and A. D. Bovopoulos, "An Access Protection Solution for Heavy Load Unfairness in DQDB," *Proceedings of IEEE INFOCOM*, 1992, pp. 190–199.

[38] M. Kabatepe and K. S. Vastola, "FDQ: The Fair Distributed Queue MAN," *Proceedings of IEEE INFOCOM*, 1992, pp. 200–209.

[39] A. R. Pach, S. Palazzo, and D. Panno, "Slot Pre-Using in IEEE 802.6 Metropolitan Area Networks," *IEEE Journal on Selected Areas in Communications*, vol. 11, no. 8, Oct. 1993, pp. 1249–1258.

[40] P. Tran-Gia and T. Stock, "Approximate Performance Analysis of the DQDB Access Protocol," *Computer Networks and ISDN Systems*, vol. 20, 1990, pp. 231–240.

[41] ——, "Modelling of the DQDB Access Protocol and Closed-Form Approximation," in G. Pujolle (ed.), *High-Capacity Local and Metropolitan Area Networks*. Berlin: Springer-Verlag, 1990, pp. 253–265.

[42] C. C. Bisdikian, "Waiting Time Analysis In a Single Buffer DQDB (802.6) Network," *IEEE Journal on Selected Areas in Communications*, vol. 8, no. 8, Oct. 1990, pp 1565–1573.

[43] W. Jing and M. Paterakis, "Message Delay Analysis of the DQDB (IEEE 802.6) Network," *Proceedings of IEEE INFOCOM*, 1992, pp. 527–535.

[44] M. Zukerman, "Queueing Performance of QPSX," in M. Bonatti (ed.), *Teletraffic Science for New Cost-effective Systems, Networks, and Services*. Amsterdam: North-Holland, 1989, pp. 575–581.

[45] H. R. Muller *et al.,* "DQMA and CRMA: New Access Schemes for Gbit/s LANs and MANs," *Proceedings of IEEE INFOCOM,* 1990, pp. 185–191.

[46] P. Jacquet and P. Muhlethaler, "Analytical Model for the High Speed Protocol DQDB," in G. Pujolle (ed.), *High-Capacity Local and Metropolitan Area Networks*. Berlin: Springer-Verlag, 1990, pp. 285–297.

[47] L. F. M. De Moraes, "Frame Delay Analysis of the DQDB Protocol," in G. Pujolle (ed.), *High-Capacity Local and Metropolitan Area Networks*. Berlin: Springer-Verlag, 1990, pp. 299–310.

[48] S. Ghani and M. Schwartz, "Comparison of DQDB and FDDI MAC Access Protocols," *Proceedings of IEEE 16th Conference on Local Computer Networks*, 1991, pp. 84–95.

[49] F. Tari and V. S. Frost, "Performance Comparison of DQDB and FDDI for Integrated Networks," *Proceedings of IEEE 16th Conference on Local Computer Networks*, 1991, pp. 96–105.

[50] M. Conti, E. Gregori, and L. Lenzini, "A Comprehensive Analysis of DQDB," *European Transactions on Telecommunication and Related Technologies*, vol. 2, no. 4, Jul./Aug., 1991, pp. 403–413.

[51] J. M. Ulm, "A Time Token Ring Local Area Network and Its Performance Characteristics," *Proceedings of 7th Conference on Local Computer Networks*, 1982, pp. 50–56.

[52] M. J. Johnson, "Proof that Timing Requirements of the FDDI Token Ring Protocol are Satisfied," *IEEE Transactions on Communications*, vol. 35, no. 6, June 1987, pp. 620–625.

[53] K. C. Sevick and M. J. Johnson, "Cycle Time Properties of the FDDI Token Ring Protocol," *IEEE Transactions on Software Engineering,*, vol. 13, no. 3, 1987, pp. 376–385.

[54] R. O. LaMaire, "FDDI Performance at 1 Gbit/s," *Proceedings of IEEE ICC*, 1991, 1043–1048.

[55] C. C. Lu and K. Y. Liu, "Delay Time Analysis of FDDI Protocols," *Proceedings of IEEE INFOCOM*, 1991, pp. 1440–1445.

[56] R. O. LaMaire and E. M. Spiegel, "FDDI Performance Analysis: Delay Approximations," *Proceedings of IEEE GLOBECOM*, 1990, pp. 1838–1845.

[57] R. O. LaMaire, "An M/G/1 Vacation Model of an FDDI Station," *IEEE Journal on Selected Areas in Communications*, vol. 9, no. 2, Feb. 1991, pp. 257–265.

[58] M. Tangemann and K. Sauer, "Performance Analysis of the Timed Token Protocol of FDDI and FDDI-II," *IEEE Journal on Selected Areas in Communications*, vol. 9, no. 2, Feb. 1991, pp. 271–278.

[59] A. P. Jayasumana and P. N. Werahera, "Performance of Fibre Distributed Data Interface Network for Multiple Classes of Traffic," *IEEE Proceedings,* Pt. E, vol. 137, no. 5, Sept. 1990, pp. 401–408.

[60] D. Karvelas and A. L. Garcia, "Performance Analysis of the Medium Access Control Protocol of the FDDI Token Ring Network," *Proceedings of IEEE GLOBECOM*, 1988, pp. 1119–1123.

[61] K. Takahashi and T. Suda, "Performance Analysis of an FDDI Local Area Network with Synchronous Traffic," *Proceedings of IEEE ICC*, 1991, pp. 1355–1361.

[62] K. Takahashi, J. B. Kim, and T. Soda, "Performance Analysis of an FDDI Local Area Network via Video and Data Traffic," *Proceedings of IEEE ICC*, 1993, pp. 1696–1702.

[63] L. F. Merakos, G. M. Exley, and C. Bisdikian, "Interconnection of Two CSMA Local Area Networks via a Bridge: Throughput-Delay Characteristics," *Proceedings of IEEE ICC*, 1987, pp. 987–991.

[64] H. Xie and L. Merakos, "Performance Evaluation of a System of In-
     terconnected CS MA/CD LANs via an N-Port Bridge," *Proceedings
     of IEEE ICC*, 1989, pp. 640–645.

[65] S. Gupta and K. W. Ross, "Performance Modeling and Optimiza-
     tion of Interconnected Ethernets," *Proceedings of IEEE INFOCOM*,
     1991, pp. 1353–1359.

Chapter 5

Emerging MAN Technologies

It is a profound error to presume that everything has been discovered; it is to take the horizon which bounds the eye for the limit of the world.
—A. M. Lemirre

The past decade has been very exciting in the telecommunications and computer industries. This decade and the next one will even be more exciting. In the standards arena, MAN technology is joining other technologies in forming the nucleus of future communications facilities. Compatibility of MANs with existing and future networks is therefore an important issue. One future network with which MAN must be compatible is the integrated services digital network (ISDN), approved in 1984 by the International Consultative Committee for Telephone and Telegraph (CCITT) to meet the stringent demands of customers in the 1990s and beyond.

The worldwide telephone infrastructure was designed over several decades around a single type of terminal, the analog telephone subset, which in most cases was developed to meet national specifications. Subsequently, technological advances made it possible to develop new terminals for various types of communication (e.g., text, facsimile, videotex) using the existing telephone network. A major objective of ISDN is to provide an infrastructure that can support these new terminal devices.

ISDN is a facility that many claim to be the most significant advance in telecommunications since the introduction of the telephone itself. Using ISDN for interconnection is becoming more and more attractive. If MAN standards are written carefully, it is possible to interconnect MANs with ISDN facilities [1]. Also, the acceptance of asynchronous transfer mode (ATM) for use in the public WANs in the form of broadband ISDN has led to the emergence of new services and technologies such as ATM LANs, frame and cell relays, and switched multimegabit data service (SMDS).

The aim of this chapter is to consider the future of MAN in relation to ISDN and related emerging services and technologies. The chapter begins with a brief introduction to the narrowband ISDN architecture in Section 5.1 and then covers broadband ISDN in Section 5.2. The following sections address ATM LANs, frame and cell relays, SONET, and SMDS. In Section 5.7, we address the future of MANs as the cornerstone in the broadband era.

5.1 Narrowband ISDN

Telecommunication services are currently provided to the customers over dedicated links for each network. The major disadvantages of this system are the duplication of resources, the complication of internetworking between the different networks, and the relative inefficiency of dividing traffic over a variety of media. It was conceived that a unified telecommunication environment capable of carrying all services would be beneficial to both operator and user. Thus the idea of integrated services was born. Planning for ISDN started in 1976.

ISDN is the first network-based standard for simultaneous integrated voice, data, and video signal transmission over a single pair of wires instead of the separate pairs formerly needed for each service. The idea of ISDN is illustrated in Figure 5.1. It evolved from the need to integrate different types of traffic into one network. The customer needs that are driving ISDN development include the following [2]:

- The need for digital communications that provide enhanced reliability, availability, and quality of transmission
- The need for higher data transmission speeds at lower costs
- The need for increased efficiency in communication systems achieved through simplicity, flexibility, and compatibility
- The need for efficient use of switching and transmission facilities
- The need for dynamic bandwidth allocations and network diagnostic capabilities

Other factors include ease of administration, cost reduction to the user, and higher data transmission speeds. As with most technologies, low cost is the major driving factor for the wide acceptance of ISDN.

5.1.1 Basic Concepts

ISDN is not itself a service, but an interface to existing and future services. Also, ISDN is not a product, but an architecture that allows communication networks to better serve the increasing demands for digital connectivity and new network services. It is an evolving international standard for voice and data communications. In fact, ISDN may be

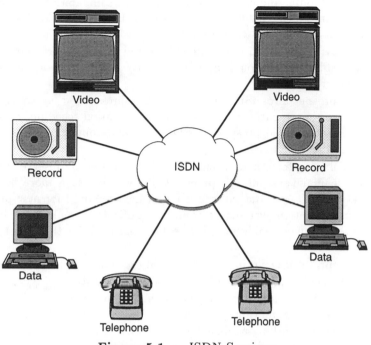

Figure 5.1   ISDN Services.

viewed as a set of recommendations from CCITT based on the concept of providing a set of channels at a single interface [3].

The major concepts of ISDN are these [4]:

- The network supports a wide range of applications (voice, data, image, video, graphics, fax, etc.).
- Using a limited number of types of connections and a small number of interfaces, the network can supply a wide range of services.
- Both packet switching and circuit switching are provided on the network.

ISDN has several advantages [5, 6]:

- It enables a single point of access for voice and data. Because it is a digital network, it is able to transmit all forms of data, text, image video, and digitized voice over a single network transparently. This is the feature that makes ISDN very attractive to users.
- Combining voice traffic and data traffic on a single network optimizes operating costs because the network uses a common set of switching and transmission facilities for both types of traffic. Current systems use separate facilities.
- It provides additional revenues from new services.
- It allows using less than 25% of the bandwidth currently required for voice communication without sacrificing quality.

- The computer and communication network companies face a dilemma of interfacing heterogeneous systems. ISDN's goal is solving this incompatibility and creating a common set of standards.
- It provides standard user connections and terminal portability, and it enables international interconnectivity due to globally accepted standards.

The prospects for ISDN services look impressive, so much so that there is growing impatience with the implementation schedule. In spite of its advantages and prospects, ISDN has many opponents. Some of their arguments follow [5–7].

- The driving force behind current ISDN plans is to preserve the investment in existing equipment while evolving to a more flexible network. Due to the enormous investment required for new public communication systems, it would be difficult to replace or duplicate the huge analog public telephone network by the new ISDN exchanges.
- The current ISDN is inherently hybrid (a combination of circuit and packet switching) that will not work satisfactorily.
- The ISDN standardization process has been in progress for more than a decade, and much is yet to be done. The standards organizations are working against the clock. Assembling a set of globally accepted standards has been difficult. There are some political, commercial, technological, and regulatory issues that will constrain the development of ISDN. Countries that operate under a regulated system, where the telecommunication system is under government control, argue for public control. The rapid advances in technology over the past decade (e.g., VLSI and fiber optics) have made ISDN standardization difficult. How can a standard be formulated when the technology is either uncertain or changing rapidly?

5.1.2 Basic Structure

In ISDN, all information is digitally encoded before transmission. With an all-digital network, voices will be transmitted at the same speeds with improved sound quality, and data will move about seven times faster.

The basic ISDN operating scheme, or interface, involves two types of channels [8, 9]:

1. The B channel (the in-band, or B for bearer, channel) carries the user's message. This is a 64-kbps channel similar to the pulse-code modulation transmission system in existing telephone network. (Note that the reason for choosing the channel size of 64 kbps is that current telephone switching systems are based on that size.) A B channel can carry voice, data or video.
2. The D channel (the out-of-band, or D for data, channel) carries primarily network-signaling or control information. It sets up calls, dis-

connects them, and properly routes data on the B channels through the network.

Fundamental to ISDN are two concepts [10]: distributed processing and out-of-band signaling. Distributed processing allows equipment to perform data processing at remote locations. This, of course, necessitates security measures to prevent unauthorized use. *Signaling* is the name given to the procedures of ISDN for creating and clearing down connections, and *out-of-band* refers to the signaling procedures, indicating that these are carried on a separate channel from voice or data [11]. Out-of-band signaling occurring on the D channel means that the channels carrying user messages are separated from channels carrying signals for controlling the network. This puts message-routing control in the hands of the customer rather than in the hands of the communications provider.

Two interfaces differing mainly in their carrying capacity, are currently defined [10, 12]. These interfaces are illustrated in Figure 5.2. The *basic rate interface* (BRI) consists of two 64-bps B channels and one 16-bps D channel. The higher-capacity *primary rate interface* (PRI) has twenty-three 64-kbps B channels and one 64-kbps D channel (i.e., 23B + D). In Europe, the primary rate interface (PRI) consists of thirty 64-kbps B channels with two D channels (i.e., 30B + 2D).

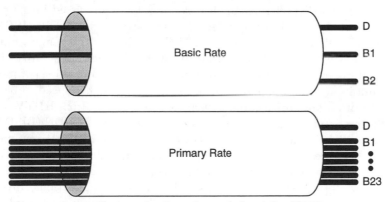

Figure 5.2   Two major interfaces defined for ISDN.

A generic architecture for the customer premises end of an ISDN interface is shown in Figure 5.3. The architecture has three primary attributes: end-to-end digital connectivity, multiple services over the same transmission path with out-of- band signaling, and standard interfaces and conversion facilities for access by users. Details of this architecture are discussed by Roca [12] and Asatani [13].

Over 60,000 circuits, mostly of the BRI type, are in use in the United States by major Fortune 500 corporations participating in ISDN field trials. Needless to say, this number would have to reach a far

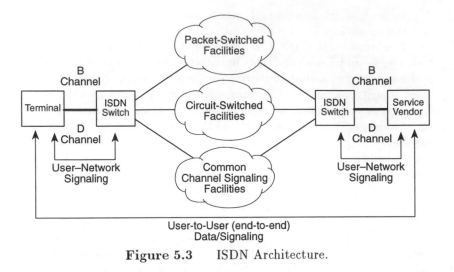

Figure 5.3   ISDN Architecture.

greater percentage to realize the true value of ISDN services. Many areas of applications of ISDN are discussed in [14, 15].

5.2 Broadband ISDN

The BRI and PRI offerings of the standard ISDN discussed in the previous section are collectively referred to as narrowband ISDN (NISDN). Thus, NISDN provides services that will be carried by channels based on 64 kbps up to 1.5 Mbps (or 2 Mbps for the European standard). The characteristics of NISDN are inadequate for many applications of interest and in meeting the perceived users' needs for higher speed, broader bandwidth, and more flexibility such as video distribution, HDTV, and HiFi stereo. These needs are accomodated in broadband ISDN (BISDN). Consequently, as far as data networks are concerned, the real excitement of ISDN comes about when one considers the capabilities of BISDN [16].

It seems appropriate to define the term *broadband.* The term is used in two ways [17]: broadband access and broadband applications. Broadband access is digital access from a subscriber's premises to a telephone company's switch via an optical fiber connection supporting a data rate greater than 2 Mbps. In other words, broadband is the provision of subscriber access at bit rates in excess of 2 Mbps. Broadband applications are those implemented through broadband access and require data rates greater than those generally available in NISDN. Figure 5.4 puts broadband in the context of other forms of communication.

The BISDN concept developed from the fact that a large range of voice, data, and video services can be simultaneously carried on the same optical system. Broadband is the provision of subscriber access at bit rates in the range of 1.5 Mbps up to approximately 150 Mbps. The

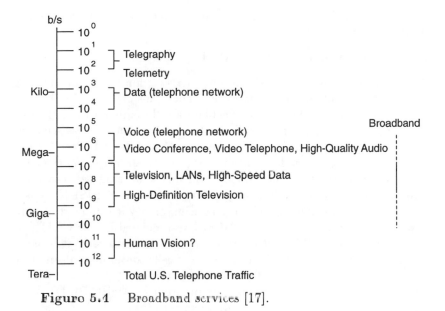

Figure 5.1 Broadband services [17].

demand for broadband communication originated from business and residential customers. Residential customers are interested in distribution services such as TV. Business customers require services for video, data, text, and graphics. The bit rates for these services are in the range of 2 to 130 Mbps and require broadband communication [18, 19]. It is foreseen that most of the needs for wideband international connection will be met by BISDN. It is therefore desirable that MANs achieve a degree of BISDN compatibility.

BISDN is regarded as an all-purpose digital network in that it will provide an integrated access that will support a wide variety of applications in a flexible and cost-effective manner. The network capabilities will include support for [20]

- Interactive and distributive services such as video conferencing, telefax, TV distribution, and so on
- Broadband and narrowband rates
- Bursty and continuous traffic
- Connection-oriented and connectionless services
- Digital signal processing
- Point-to-point and complex communications such as multimedia applications. (A multimedia application is one that can include several different types of media such as audio, video, encoded text, raster and vector graphics, image data, and control data. Typical areas of multimedia application include desktop publishing, flight reservation, investment banking, advertising, research, graphic arts, and entertainment.)

The goal of BISDN is to provide a user interface and network that will meet these varied requirements.

5.2.1 Asynchronous Transfer Mode

A transfer mode usually refers to both the switching and multiplexing aspects of a communication network. The transfer mode for BISDN must be able to handle both narrowband and broadband rates, handle both continuous and bursty traffic, satisfy delay- and/or loss-sensitive quality requirements, and meet unforeseen demands [21]. Neither circuit mode nor packet mode is suitable for meeting all these requirements. Asynchronous transfer mode (ATM), which is something between these two modes, has been selected as the target solution of BISDN. It is a specific packet oriented transfer mode using an asynchronous time- division multiplexing technique. ATM has been defined by the CCITT as a transfer mode in which information is organized into cells; it is asynchronous in the sense that the recurrence of cells containing information from an individual user is not necessarily periodic.

ATM may be regarded as the foundation on which BISDN is to be built. The term *asynchronous* distinguishes the mode from the synchronous transfer mode (STM), which predominates in today's switched networks. Synchronous switching (also known as circuit switching) allows messages to be sent in a prescribed time schedule, whereas in asynchronous switching messages are sent at any desired time. In STM-based networks, information is organized in periodic time slots for the duration of a call as in Figure 5.5(a). The rule for subdivision and allocation of bandwidth using STM is simple: Allocate time slots within a recurring structure (frame) to a service for the duration of a call. Thus, STM techniques require the dedication of time slots to individual services. They are well suited for networks supporting fixed-rate services. They inefficiently support bursty data traffic and do not easily support the range of service bit rates required for BISDN. A high-speed network is inherently asynchronous because it is very hard to perform synchronization at high speeds. Also, asynchronous switching is flexible and can use network resources dynamically [22].

ATM does not necessarily have periodic time slots assigned to a channel. In ATM networks, information is organized in fixed-size segments (or slots) called *cells*, which may appear at irregular intervals as illustrated in Figure 5.5(b). Each cell consists of a header and an information field. Using the ATM technique, the information stream of each service is packetized and placed in short fixed-length cells. These cells must be reasonably short for at least two reasons: (1) in order to reduce the degrading effect of the packetization delay at the source, and (2) to meet the requirements of the most critical services, such as real-time video.

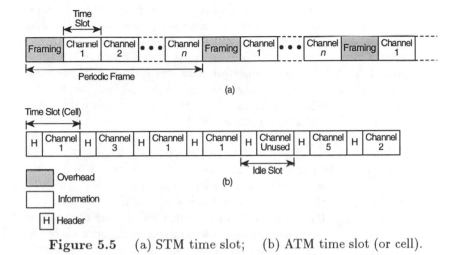

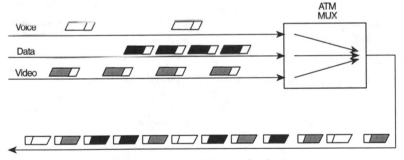

Figure 5.5   (a) STM time slot;   (b) ATM time slot (or cell).

ATM is a connection-oriented technique. As a result, delay variation is minimized because cells belonging to the same call follow the same route. The techique also minimizes the processing required to make routing decisions. The ATM technique allows efficient sharing of the transmission medium by using the ATM cell as a multiplexing unit as illustrated in Figure 5.6. Cell multiplexing is also more flexible than the familiar time-division multiplexing because it can work regardless of the time position of cells [23, 24].

Figure 5.6   ATM multiplexing.

As shown in Figure 5.7, an ATM cell consists of a 40-bit (5-octet) header field and a 384-bit (48-octet) information that contains user data. The header field contains all the necessary information for routing the cell through the ATM network and performs the following functions: flow control, virtual channel identification, cell loss detection, and error control [25, 26]. The header format used at the user–network interface (UNI) is shown in Figure 5.8. The fields in the header are described as follows:

- *Generic Flow Control* (GFC): This is a 4-bit field used to determine the priority of cells. It assists the customer premises in controlling the flow of traffic for different qualities of service.
- *Virtual Path Identifier* (VPI): This consists of 8 bits and is part of 24-bit label field for the connection identifier for the ATM network. A virtual path is a essentially a bundle of virtual circuits that are switched as a unit by defining one additional layer of multiplexing on a per-cell basis underneath the VCI.
- *Virtual Channel Identifier* (VCI): This consists of the remaining 16 bits of the label field for the connection identifier. A virtual channel is a logical connection between two users. Whereas the VPI provides an explicit circuit identification for a cell, the VCI provides an explicit circuit identification for a cell.
- *Payload Type* (PT): A 2-bit field that indicates whether the payload contains user information or network maintenance information. The PT field allows for the insertion of cells onto a virtual channel without impacting the user's data.
- *Reserved* (R): This 1-bit field is reserved for future use.
- *Cell Loss Priority* (C): A 1-bit field used by the user to indicate the cell's priority. One possible implementation is to set $C = 1$ for cells that are droppable and $C = 0$ for cells that need guaranteed delivery. When congestion occurs, cells with $C = 1$ are dropped first.
- *Header Error Control* (HEC): This is an 8-bit error check field that monitors the errors for the entire header. The HEC provides single-bit error correction or multiple-bit error detection capabilities on the cell header. The polynomial used to generate the header error check value is

$$G(x) = x^8 + x^2 + x + 1 \tag{5.1}$$

which is the same as that used for DQDB (see Eq. (3.2)).

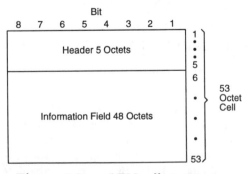

Figure 5.7   ATM cell structure.

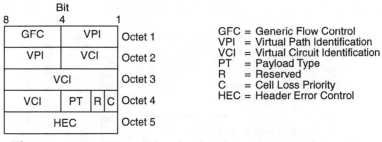

Figure 5.8 ATM cell header for the user–network interface.

The label is theoretically the only field that is required in the ATM cell header for switching and multiplexing functions. However, other considerations, some related to enhanced performance, warrant the inclusion of other fields. The header format for the UNI shown in Figure 5.8 is the same for the network-node interface (NNI) except that for the NNI, the header does not contain a GFC field, so the extra 4 bits are used for a VPI field.

It should be noted that there are some doubts about the suitability and economy of ATM as a universal transfer mode for all kinds of services. Due to this, the option of an STM-based interface is being maintained within CCITT.

Table 5.1 **Sublayers of the BISDN Protocol Layers.**

	Higher layers
Adaptation Layer	Convergence sublayer
	Segmentation and Reassembly sublayer
ATM Layer	Virtual Channel sublayer
	Virtual Path sublayer
Physical Layer	Transmission Convergence sublayer
	Physical Medium sublayer

5.2.2 Protocol Reference Model

The BISDN protocol structure is shown in Figure 5.9. The sublayers are shown in Table 5.1. The physical layer, the ATM layer, and the ATM

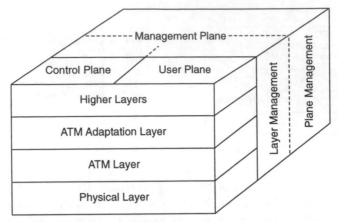

Figure 5.9   BISDN protocol reference model.

adaptation layer (AAL) can be regarded as layer 1 and part of layer 2 of the corresponding OSI seven-layer model [13, 26–28].

The physical layer consists of two sublayers: the physical medium sublayer, which mainly transmits the bits, and the transmission convergence sublayer which transforms cells into data over a physical medium. For the physical medium, coaxial cable and optical fibers are serious contenders. Coaxial cable may be used for distances up to 200 m, and optical fiber may be used for up to 2 km. Twisted pair is another important medium for ATM carrier. In addition to the physical medium, the physical layer also includes the framing structure. Two alternatives have been identified: the pure ATM-based structure and the SDH-based structure. In the first, the physical medium receives a continuous stream of ATM cells from the ATM layer; in the second, the ATM cell streams are routed as tributaries within a frame based on the synchronous digital hierarchy (SDH).

The ATM layer addresses the ATM cell structure and coding. It provides cell multiplexing and demultiplexing functions. The layer is divided into two sublayers: virtual channel and virtual path sublayers. The virtual channel sublayer performs routing of the ATM cells and ensures that the cell flow does not violate the limits specified during the call setup phase. A virtual path is a set of multiplex circuits that terminate at common end nodes such as switching nodes or gateways. Two fundamental principles characterize the ATM layer: (1) This layer is common to all services, providing cell transfer capabilities, and (2) the boundary between ATM layer and adaptation layer corresponds to the boundary between the functions devoted to the cell header and the functions related to the information field. In view of these points, the ATM layer has to be as versatile and flexible as possible to cope with the variety of services to be conveyed on ATM channels. The characteristics of the ATM layer are independent of the physical medium. Although ATM is the target transfer mode, the synchronous optical network (SONET) will provide the target transmission infrastructure.

The ATM adaptation layer (AAL) lies between the ATM layer and higher layers. Its role is to map or adapt the functions or services supported by the higher layers onto a common ATM bearer service. It is needed to support information-transfer protocols not based on ATM. Thus, AAL functions are service dependent. The AAL performs functions required by the user, control, and management planes. It is divided into two different logical sublayers: the convergence sublayer and the segmentation and reassembly sublayer. The convergence sublayer provides the AAL service to higher layers and is service dependent. The segmentation and reassembly layer performs segmentation of long messsages at the sending end and reassembling into messages at the receiving end.

The proposed IEEE 802.6 MAN standard is defined as an interconnection of the distributed-queue dual-bus (DQDB) subnetworks. The IEEE MAN has unique characteristics and service definitions that correspond to those adopted for BISDN. The close relationship between the IEEE MAN and BISDN became apparent only over a period of time. Although the IEEE MAN architecture's cell is also 53 octets divided into a 5-octet header and a 48-octet field, it is not called an ATM cell. The MAN has a physical layer designed to be medium independent to allow for future transmission media and rates. To date, the IEEE MAN and BISDN have the following commonalities [29]:

1. Support of connection-oriented and connectionless services
2. Transfer of information in cells over asynchronous virtual channels
3. Use of uniform format cells for all services

Table 5.2 compares IEEE 802.6 with BISDN. Although some differences remain, the IEEE 802.6 standard and BISDN standard are currently aligned so as to facilitate the provision of a common family of interfaces. Thus, the DBDQ subnetwork can be the evolutionary path toward BISDN.

5.2.3 Applications and Services

Broadband applications are any end uses of the broadband network capabilities. Typical applications include LAN interconnection, video telephony, and video conferencing. Broadband services are the facilities that a network provides to support broadband applications via a BISDN. In particular, a network capability (service) may be used by many applications.

Broadband ISDN will offer a family of services and provide a wide range of end user applications with varying requirements on throughput,

Table 5.2   Comparison of IEEE 802.6 and BISDN [30].

Features	IEEE 802.6	BISDN
Services	Data and voice	Data, voice, and video
Goals	Architecture	Interface/services
Geographical scope	50 km	Global
Topology	Ring/bus	Double-star
Speed	45, 100, 150 Mbps	150–600 Mbps
Connection mode	Isochronous: connection oriented Nonisochronous: connectionless and connection oriented	Connection oriented
Transfer mode	Isochronous: connection-oriented Nonisochronous: connectionless	ATM
Ownership	Public/private	Public/private
Compatibility	IEEE 802 LANs	Narrowband ISDN

Table 5.3   Broadband services and applications.

Services	Applications	Bandwidth
High-speed transmission	Large file transfer LAN interconnect	1–100 Mbps
Video distribution	HDTV CATV	50–135 Mbps
Video telephony	General video telephony Picture mail	Up to 150 Mbps
Video conferencing	TV conferencing Workstation conference	Up to 150 Mbps

delay, variation in delay, and reconfiguration intervals. A multitude of potential broadband applications and services have been proposed for the broadband network [15, 17, 31–35]. A few examples of the broadband services are shown in Table 5.3. The services can be divided into two categories: high-speed data services and video services.

The high-speed data services include those the large corporate customers may require such as for the interconnection of LANs, file transfer, remote computer aided design, and manufacturing applications. Immediate needs for the interconnection of LANs and terminals over local, metropolitan, national, and international distances are growing as many companies become more dispersed while they are increasingly dependent on shared data. Narrowband data services will be severely strained in meeting the developing needs of growing numbers of computer users in the coming decade. Video services can be divided into three broad categories: interactive/communicative, retrieval, and distributive services. The first is two-way with essentially symmetric services; the last two are essentially one-way services. Interactive services involve an exchange of information between the originating subscriber and the service object. Retrieval services entail the extraction of stored information from a database. Distributive services have an essentially passive "entertainment" quality. Specific video services include broadband video telephony and video conferencing, video surveillance, high-resolution-image services, video mail services, broadband videotex, broadband movie distribution, and electronic movie distribution. For example, TV conferencing captures the spirit of a live, interactive conference. Video transmission services are now being offered for road traffic monitoring, patient monitoring in hospitals, and security services such as telesupervision. Figure 5.10 displays the broadband service bit rates; Figure 5.11 illustrates the evolution of broadband services in the United States. Though we expect that high-speed data services will represent the initial market drive for broadband service, in the longer term video services will dominate the broadband ISDN capacity requirements.

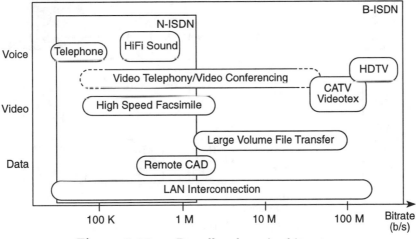

Figure 5.10   Broadband service bit rates.

BISDN is being driven into existence by both market pull and a technology push, but as a new technology, BISDN needs to be perfected by standards bodies, researchers, developers, and implementers. Nevertheless, a set of new concepts, services, and technologies have evolved from the development of BISDN. Some of these services and technologies are discussed in the following sections. More details on ISDN are available from the IEEE Proceedings [36].

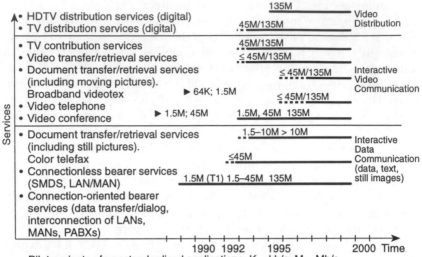

Pilot projects of nonstandardized applications: K = kb/s; M = Mb/s.

Figure 5.11   Evolution of broadband services in the United States.

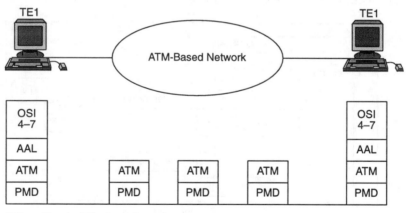

TE   = Terminal Equipment
PMD = Physical Medium Dependent

Figure 5.12   A typical ATM network.

5.3 ATM LANs

The ATM LAN is one of the emerging ATM networks. ATM networks were initially envisioned to be a transport technology for delivering integrated services on the public WANs in the form of BISDN. A typical ATM network is shown in Figure 5.12, where the terminal equipments (TEs) might be LANs, high-speed host computers, or CAD/CAM workstations. An ATM network allows the flexible allocation of bandwidth for packet, circuit-switched, or dedicated services. The potential benefits of this technology have led to its acceptance as a local networking technology. ATM in the local area has many forms. Shared media ATM networks include DQDB, the Cambridge Fast Ring, the Cambridge Backbone Ring, and the Orwell Ring.

Two important considerations make the ATM LAN different from the public BISDN. First, cost is the key consideration in the local network. Economics and deployment in the local and public networks are vastly different, even from time- scale consideration alone. Overprovision of bandwidth may be the key to reducing the cost of local area ATM. Second, reliability in the local network is turning out to be an increasingly important consideration. General topology networks allow a continuum of tradeoffs between cost and fault tolerance. Reliability in the local network must be configurable.

ATM provides significant advantages to both end users and network operators, including the following [37]:

- Support of a wide variety of connection rates
- Flexible synchronization techniques
- Service integration
- New flexible network architecture

Although ATM provides these advantages, it presents a number of challenges. First, voice service places strict delay requirements on ATM-based networks. Second, momentary overloads, as are possible with bursty traffic, could cause overflow in buffers in the ATM switches and loss of cells. To effectively support bursty services, some means of congestion control is needed. Third, ATM has a great susceptibility to transmission errors. Bit errors in the header of an ATM cell could cause the loss of an entire cell.

The consideration of local wireless ATM networks highlights the requirement to consider and specify ATM service in a manner that is not based on a particular implementation. A wireless network that aims to provide an ATM service must provide a solution to the duplication and sequencing problem just below the ATM level.

The ATM offers the possibility of unifying communications. The unification goes beyond interconnecting LANs and WANs. ATM facilitates unification along the following three dimensions [38]:

- *Service:* A wide range of upper-layer services are supported by a single transfer mechanism.
- *Operating Environments:* ATM can be used in wired or wireless environments, in private or public networks, and in a wide range of localities and bandwidths.
- *Administrative Domain Interconnection:* The separation of the network transfer and policy mechanism (governing routing, security, etc.) facilitates the efficient interconnection of administrative domain.

5.4 SONET

The synchronous optical network (SONET) is a fiber-optics-based network for use by telephone companies [39]. SONET provides an open standard optical interface for transmission at the broadband user-network and between network nodes. It is an emerging technology that will definitely have an impact on MANs and MAN services.

SONET was originally proposed by Bellcore (Bell Communication Research) as a standard optical interface. It is now an ANSI standard that defines a high-speed digital hierarchy for optical fiber. An international version of SONET is the synchronous digital hierarchy (SDH).

SONET is not a communications network in the same sense as a LAN or MAN. Rather, it is an underlying transport network over which communications networks such as FDDI, IEEE DQDB, and SMDS can all operate. SONET then provides the basis for the optical infrastucture that will be necessary to meet the communications of the decade and beyond.

The four optical interface layers for SONET are shown in Figure 5.13. They correspond to the physical layer of the OSI model. The layers, from the bottom up, are as follows:

- *Photonic layer:* This is mainly responsible for converting electrical signals to optical signals. The layer handles the transmission of bits across the optical fiber.
- *Section layer:* This is responsible for transmitting STS-N frames (to be discussed later) across the transmission medium. Other functions include framing, scrambling, and error monitoring.
- *Line layer:* This handles the transmission of path layer overhead and payload across the medium. It is also responsible for synchronization and multiplexing for the path layer.
- Path layer: This essentially maps services into the format required by the line layer for transmission over the fiber. A path corresponds to a logical connection between source and destination.

In SONET, the basic unit of transport is called the *synchronous transport signal level 1* (STS-1) frame, which has a bit rate of 51.84 Mbps and repeats every 125 μs (i.e., 8,000 SONET frames are generated per second). An STS-1 frame structure is portrayed in Figure 5.14. It consists of 9 rows and 90 columns (9 × 90 bytes, forming a total of 810 bytes per frame). Each rectangle in Figure 5.14 represents a 125 μs snapshot of a transmission signal. Transmission occurs from left to right, row by row.

As also shown in Figure 5.14, the STS-1 frame is divided into two areas known as the *transport overhead* (TOH) and the *synchronous payload envelope* (SPE). The TOH carries overhead information, and the SPE carries the SONET payload, which may be ATM based or STM based.

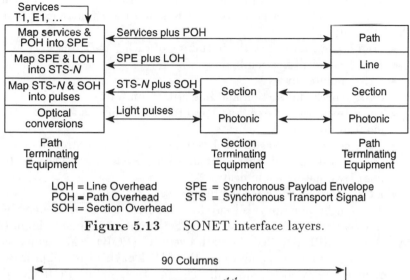

LOH = Line Overhead   SPE = Synchronous Payload Envelope
POH = Path Overhead   STS = Synchronous Transport Signal
SOH = Section Overhead

Figure 5.13   SONET interface layers.

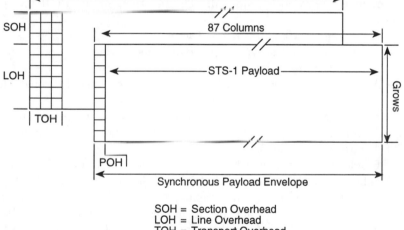

SOH = Section Overhead
LOH = Line Overhead
TOH = Transport Overhead
POH = Path Overhead

Figure 5.14   STS-1 frame structure.

The transport overhead (TOH) basically carries information required to secure transmission for the SPE. The TOH consists of the first 3 columns (3×9 bytes) of an STS-1 frame. It can be divided into two parts: the section overhead (SOH), which is the first 3 rows (3×3 bytes), and the line overhead (LOH), which is the last 6 rows (3×6 bytes). The SOH is processed at each generator; it provides such functions as framing and bit-error detection. The LOH is passed transparently through regenerators and is processed by light-wave terminating equipment; it provides services that include a pointer to the actual beginning of the payload within the frame. The transport overhead carries overhead bits for connections at both the section level and the line level. The transport overhead bits and their functions include the following [40]:

- Framing bytes to show the beginning of each STS-1 frame
- An STS-1 identification byte
- STS-1 pointer bytes
- Parity checks for section and line error monitoring
- Local (section) and express (line) orderwire channels for voice communication between elements
- Data communication channels for maintenance, control, monitor, administration, and other communication needs between section (or line) terminating equipments
- Extra bytes reserved for the future use

The synchronous payload envelope (SPE) occupies the remaining 87 columns (= 87×9 bytes) of the STS-1 frame. The first column (9 bytes) of the SPE is called the path overhead (POH), which is passed transparently from the point where the STS-1 payload is composed to the point where it is decomposed. The functions of the POH include these:

- End-to-end payload error monitoring
- Identification of the type of payload being carried
- Path status indication
- A trace function, which allows a user to trace a signal through the network as it goes through different elements

The remaining 86 columns of the SPE are used to carry the service or signal being transported. After all the overheads are accomodated, the STS-1 data rate is 49.536 Mbps.

Besides the STS-1, which serves as the basic building block, there are higher rate SONET signals (STS-N). An STS-N channel rate is obtained by synchronously mutiplexing N STS-1 inputs. An STS-N frame has $90 \times N$ columns per row, including $4 \times N$ columns of interface overhead. An STS-3, for example, is formed by octet-interleaving three STS-1 frames. Standards already define rates from STS-1 (51.84 Mbps) to STS-48 (2.48832 Gbps), as shown in Table 5.4, where optical carrier level N (OC-N) is the optical equivalent of an STS-N electrical signal. The standard will eventually define rates up to STS-255 (13.2192 Gbps).

SONET offers cross-connect capabilities that can be used to transport aggregations of ATM connections within the network. Its synchronous multiplexing capabilities can be used to combine several ATM streams to build interfaces at rates greater than those supported by the ATM layer. SONET is capable of transporting a wide variety of data stream types regardless of the data formats or rates. It can be used to carry either ATM-based or STM-based payloads, making it possible to initially deploy a high-capacity fiber-based transmission infrastructure for aggregated narrowband and data services.

The work on SONET standards continues as some open issues are being resolved. SONET will find applications in BISDN, FDDI, and SMDS. As optic technology takes a greater share of the transmission market, SONET multiplexing equipment will be installed to provide transmission at 51.840 Mbps or its multiples. This will pave the way for BISDN. For now, the two important SONET rates for BISDN are the STS-3 (155.52 Mbps) and STS-12 (622.08 Mbps). Later, the SONET STS-24 (1.2 Gbps) and STS-48 (2.4 Gbps) rates will be important. Needless to say, SONET will play a significant role, both economically and technologically, in the evolution toward broadband. ATM and SONET together depict a suitable combination for the transport and delivery of information in the broadband network.

Table 5.4   **SONET optical carriers.**

SONET Level	Line Rate (Mbps)
OC-1	51.84
OC-3	155.52
OC-9	466.56
OC-12	622.08
OC-18	933.12
OC-24	1244.16
OC-36	1866.24
OC-48	2488.32

5.5 Frame and Cell Relays

Frame and cell relays are new switching techniques that have grown out of ISDN standards [41]. Frame relay is a packet-mode, connection-oriented, link-layer service that provides unacknowledged transfer of frames between users at access speeds of up to 2 Mbps.

Frame relay is based on a data-link-layer protocol used in ISDN known as LAPD (link-access procedure for D channel). Data link protocols have been designed to detect and correct errors and usually operate on every link in the connection. However, due to the move to digital transmission and switching systems, the bit error rates have dropped dramatically, thereby eliminating the need to correct errors at every link. Instead, it is now feasible to perform the link layer function on an end-to-end basis. Thus, by applying this end-to-end linking approach in a frame relay network, a node may forward some part of a frame while still receiving it, obviously streamlining the transmission process. The concept of forwarding a frame while still receiving it is generally referred to as *fast packet switching.* The main differences between conventional packet switching (used in X.25) and fast packet switching are summarized in Table 5.5. Fast packet switching is a technique common to ATM, frame relay, and SMDS. As illustrated in Figure 5.15, ATM and SMDS have a fixed-size frame called a cell whereas frame relay allows a variable-size frame. (Both SMDS and BISDN are cell relay techniques.) Fast packet switching is used in supporting the very high-speed and reliable fiber optic transmission facilities.

Table 5.5   Comparison of conventional and fast packet switching techniques.

Feature	Conventional Packet Switching	Fast Packet Switching	Result
Bottleneck	Link bandwidth	Switch bandwidth	Use of optical fibers and need for fast switching
Protocol	Complex	Simple	Link error recovery is not required
Packet length	Variable	Fixed and short	Less delay, less jitter (variance of delay), and less buffer management complexity
Switching	In software	In hardware	Higher speeds
Error control	Link-to-link basis	End-to-end basis	Less processing overhead at switching nodes

Frame relay can be thought of as the next step after X.25. It has lower processing overhead than earlier forms of packet switching. Consequently, frame relay data travels much faster (at rates of 1.544 Mbps and higher) than X.25 data. In a sense, frame relay falls between lower-speed dial-up modem and packet networks, combining some advantages of both. Like a dedicated line, frame relay operates at high data rates. Like an X.25 or dial-up network, it offers the ability to connect multiple sites cheaply, allocating adequate bandwidth to each site.

In a frame relay, the user's data is transported as a series of variable length LAPD frames that are relayed from switch to switch through the network until they reach their destination. Error correction is not performed by the network. If required, it is performed on an end-to-end basis by the terminal equipment.

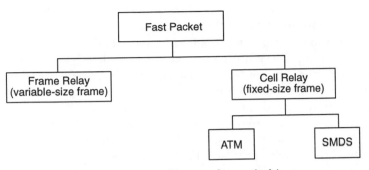

Figure 5.15   Fast packet switching.

Frame relaying has been standardized by CCITT and ANSI as an emerging data service for ISDN. It provides a balance between functionality and speed that is suitable for bridging LAN and WAN. Frame relay networks simplify the switching process by moving the procedures for recovery from error and congestion from within the network to the network periphery.

The network functions that can be accessed by a user in a frame relay service are called *core functions*, which include the following [42]:

- Frame delimiting, alignment, and transparency
- Frame multiplexing/demultiplexing using the address field, specifically the data link connection identifier
- Frame inspection to ensure that the frame consists of an integer number of octets and is neither too long nor too short
- Detection of transmission errors

With these functions, frame relaying has the following properties:

- Preservation of the order of frame transfer from one edge of the network to the other
- Nonduplication of frames
- A small probability of frame loss

The two application areas most cited for frame relay are electronic imaging and LAN interconnection. These applications are characterized by bursty traffic with occasional large file transfer rather than a steady flow of data.

Frame relay works well in image transmission because of its ability to handle high-bandwidth bursts of data. Potential users of imaging applications range from insurance companies transmitting facsimiles of claims forms to manufacturers that want to transmit product photos.

Frame relaying is potentially suitable as interconnecting (remote) bridges for at least three reasons. First, the access speeds of up to 2 Mbps are suitable. Second, the protocol overheads can be very low, thereby allowing bridges to use the high access speeds. Third, the high-speed access can be more cost-effective because it can be shared by multiple logical links. Also, since the size of the frames can vary, it is possible to allocate bandwidth dynamically on demand.

As a wide area interface and potential public service, frame relay promises to improve WAN performance, streamline interconnects, use bandwidth more efficiently, and reduce overall equipment cost. As illustrated in Figure 5.16, frame relay promises nothing less than a new architecture for a wide area with an interconnecting device. Given its strength, frame relay may well be the dominant WAN force in years to come, allowing users to abandon the dedicated, point-to- point links that dominate today's primitive LAN interconnects [43].

Although some corporations see frame relay as an economical transport method for imaging and LAN interconnection, the technology faces challenges that could stall its acceptance. Competing technologies such as BISDN and SMDS may deliver even more bandwidth for less cost. In spite of this, frame relay offers high dedicated-line speeds in a multipoint network, an important improvement over existing services [44].

Although frame relaying has great potential for LAN interconnection, it is not revolutionary but evolutionary. It is basically a simple way of getting the most out the existing high-level data link control (HDLC) technology. It can be implemented today using existing hardware and software. It can provide an evolution path to the higher speeds required in tomorrow's world.

Cell relay differs from frame relay in that fixed-size cells, rather than variable-size packets, are transmitted. It is a fast- packet-switching technology for packets with fixed-length units of data or cells. With these fixed-size cells, it is easier to integrate data, voice, and video in packet switching. Variations to end-to-end delay (jitter) are easily controlled because voice and video are sensitive to such variations. Because fixed-size cells can be handled more efficiently than variable-sized packets, a cell relay switch would probably offer lower per-bit transmission costs than a frame relay switch.

Cell relay technology is easy to design into products. It is an ideal technology for integrated broadband transport of data, voice, and video services, and could meet the needs of the telecommunications industry for higher-speed ISDN capabilities. To address these needs, the IEEE, ANSI, and CCITT are developing standards for cell-relay-based networks. The first standard is the IEEE 802.6 MAN standard for cell relay data transport and switching rates from 1.544 through 155 Mbps.

5.6 SMDS

The 64-kbps-based ISDN may not meet the delay requirements expected by LAN customers. Moreover, the LAN to ISDN access protocol adaptation necessary for supporting LAN interconnectivity by 64-kbps-based

ISDN is complex and presents a severe performance bottleneck [45]. There is a need for a high-speed, connectionless data service that provides both high transmission speed, low delay, and a simple, efficient protocol adaptation for LAN interconnection [46, 47]. This connectionless data service is called *switched multisegment data service* (SMDS) in the United States and *connectionless broadband data service* (CBDS) in Europe [48].

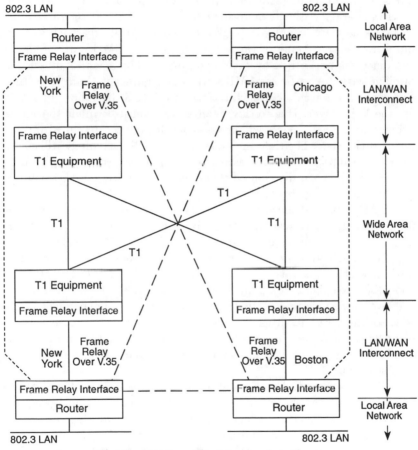

Figure 5.16   Frame relay interface.

SMDS was developed by Bell Communications Research (Bellcore), the research arm of the seven Bell regional holding companies [49]. The motivation for SMDS is fourfold:

1. To provide LAN-like service features over a larger geographical area. It is meant to ease the bottleneck between LANs and WANs by providing high bandwidth over a wide area

2. To provide a connectionless, high speed packet service

3. To ease integration of the service within existing customer internetworking and distributed applications environment

4. To extend the use of distributed applications

Once SMDS is fully developed, users will be able to create national or
international high-speed WANs using SMDS switches.

5.6.1 Basic Features

SMDS is a connectionless, public, packet-switched data service. It offers
services characteristically equivalent to a LAN MAC. It operates much
the same as a LAN, but over a greater geographical area with a larger
number of users. Many of the service features of SMDS are similar to
the functions performed by LAN equipment. This enables subscribers
familiar with LANs to use SMDS without significant changes to their
communication architecture. Interfaces to SMDS, like those of LANs,
are the MAC layer. Due to this, changes that must be made to routers,
bridges, and other devices will be less complicated compared with interfacing with ISDN. The tight integration with LAN technology will enable
SMDS to support wide area extensions of popular and emerging LAN
applications, such as distributed client-server computing, high-resolution
graphics, and image processing.

SMDS takes advantage of the hardware technology being developed
for the IEEE MAN standard (DQDB). Users connect to the network
using access link facilities ranging in speed from T1 (1.544 Mbps) to
T3 (44.736 Mbps), depending on their data communication needs. This
flexibility of access rates, coupled with a sharing of the 45 Mbps or
155 Mbps telephone company backbone facilities, allows users define
the level of service they want to pay for somewhat independent of the
speed of the access facilities. This is a departure from the current access
technology for private lines, where the user pays for the entire facility
bandwidth, independent of use, and pays for that bandwidth from source
to destination [41].

SMDS is not a technology but a service. This service offers features
like bit-rate access classes, address verification and screening, group addressing, full destination addressing, multicasting, routing, switching,
and so on. The MAC-level interface, called the SMDS interface protocol
(SIP), is based on the IEEE 802.6 standard for MAN. This makes SMDS
compatible with BISDN. The SIP provides the equivalent of the MAC
and physical layers. Consistent with the IEEE 802.6 MAC standard,
SMDS can transport information packets of any size up to 9,188 bytes,
meaning that that size data unit can be handled without fragmentation.
Since SMDS is a connectionless service and is designed to handle bursty
sources, it can statistically share the access transport facilites with other
services.

5.6.2 SMDS Interface Protocol

From an internetworking perspective, SMDS is a subnetwork, (i.e., one of many networks to be interconnected to provide a path between the end users). To connect to SMDS and benefit from its service, a device at the user's premises must do two things: It must be physically connected to SMDS, and it must frame the data in a format recognizable to SMDS. These two functions correspond to layers with the SMDS Interface Protocol (SIP).

Figure 5.17 shows a typical SMDS network, connecting two end systems. The LAN is connected to the SMDS via a router. The host is connected to the SMDS via the SIP, which contains three protocol layers that describes the network services and how the users get access to these services. The SIP also defines the frame structure, addressing, error control, and data transport.

The SIP is a three-layer protocol corresponding to the physical and MAC layers of the IEEE 802 standards. The three levels are described as follows [50, 51]:

- Level 1: This protocol describes the SMDS access path. The specifications currently support T1 and T3; it is hoped that SONET transmission rates will be incorporated in the future.
- Level 2: This protocol deals with the access control mechanism. It uses the same MAC scheme as DQDB for queue arbitrated access in support of connectionless data service.
- Level 3: This accepts data from higher-layer protocols.

Physical and electrical connection to the SMDS corresponds to SIP Level 1, the lowest level. SIP Levels 2 and 3 handle the addressing, framing, and other protocol processing.

5.6.3 SMDS and Other Technologies

Some of the requirements SMDS places on a broadband network include the following [45]:

- *Performance:* Since SMDS is meant to provide LAN-like capabilities over a large geographical area, a broadband network supporting SMDS is required to meet tight end-to-end delay and error requirements. SMDS has stringent objectives for speed and accuracy. At 45 Mbps across a metropolitan area, a 9-kbyte packet should reach its destination in no more than 20 milliseconds. The error threshold is five in 10^{13} delivered packets.
- *Control:* Since customer throughput requirements are diverse, the broadband network will need to implement an access control mechanism to limit the average rate at which SMDS customers can send or receive information.
- *Switching and Processing:* The SMDS functions will place challenging demands on the switching and processing entities within the

network. The entities must be capable of high throughput because SMDS subscribers may transmit at rates up to 155 Mbps.

- *Operations Support:* The operations systems suporting SMDS are a convenient way to collect, process, store, and disseminate the customer usage information.

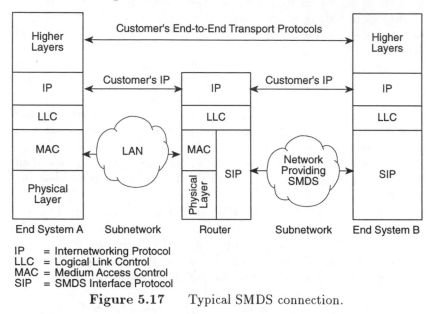

IP　　= Internetworking Protocol
LLC　= Logical Link Control
MAC = Medium Access Control
SIP　= SMDS Interface Protocol

Figure 5.17　　　Typical SMDS connection.

Compared with other competing high-speed technologies (such as FDDI and frame relay) being touted for communication networks, SMDS holds some critical advantages [48]. Unlike FDDI, SMDS has no theoretical distance limitation. FDDI's use of tokens limits the perimeter of the FDDI ring to about 60 miles, as the time taken for a token to go around a larger ring causes unacceptable delays. Although the installation of FDDI requires obtaining the right of way to install fiber lines, SMDS requires relatively few changes to customer equipment. The data rate of FDDI (100 Mbps) does not match any of the standardized public transmission rates, whereas SMDS is based on standard public network speeds. FDDI will probably be used for high-speed LANs and will complement SMDS rather than compete with it. SMDS will provide the wide area link between LANs.

Frame relay is more limited than SMDS. Frame relay is a connection-oriented point-to-point service, and its variable-length frames do not support isochronous traffic. Frame relay can improve the use of bandwidth on T1 leased lines, but it is uncertain at the moment whether it will grow beyond T1 applications. SMDS already works at T3 speeds and will accomodate data rates of 150 Mbps or higher when SONET service is fully established.

The difference between BISDN and SMDS lies mainly in the access mechanism and type of switching. BISDN will use SONET access and ATM switching: SMDS will use IEEE 802.6 switching and DS-1 or DS-3 access. Both technologies are cell relay techniques and support higher data rates than frame relay.

SMDS represents the first broadband service to make use of MAN standard and technologies. It is an important service in an evolving network interconnection strategy. One of its main deficiencies is the lack of support for isochronous services.

The common applications for SMDS include LAN interconnection and workstation-to-server and host-to-host communication. Any data service requiring high speed data transfer, such as imaging, computer aided design, publishing, and financial applications, can benefit from SMDS.

5.7 MAN Evolution Process

Figure 5.18 puts metropolitan area networks in the context of the evolution scenario of communication networks. Like other emerging technologies and services, MANs are still evolving in data rate, topology, standards development, and above all access mechanism, to name but a few aspects [52]. The evolution of MANs can be viewed from both the marketing and technology perspectives [53]. From the marketing perspective, the evolution process will take the following four stages:

- *Early Availability:* This stage provides a means of establishing awareness of MAN services.
- *SMDS Deployment:* A complete set of SMDS services will be available to customers at this stage.
- *Early Availability of Isochronous Services:* In this stage, a limited set of isochronous services will be provided.
- *MAN Integrated Service:* This is when MANs will provide full voice, data, image, and video services in an integrated form over a metropolitan area.

From the technology perspectives, MANs will evolve as the technology matures and as the underlying standard activities are developed and finalized. The technological evolution from analog to digital will continue to lead to the development of multimedia service capability in networks. Larger corporations will require high speed services. Thus, the evolution of MANs will consist of several evolutionary steps driven by technological advances, service demands, and progress in standards development.

FDDI and DQDB/SMDS are the two dominant transport standards for MANs. These will be important players in the evolution process. With SMDS representing the first broadband service defined to make use of MAN standards and technologies, MANs will in turn perform several vital functions in the broadband era. MANs will provide broadband services within a metropolitan area. They will also act as concentrators, collecting and integrating broadband traffic from a number of customers.

Internetworking between MANs and other communication networks will evolve over time as the capabilities of both MANs and other network components evolve. The initial application areas for MAN services will make use of connectionless data services, followed by connection-oriented isochronous and statistical services [54]. It seems that MANs will allow the introduction of high speed, integrated communication services to regional areas in the near future, much before ATM will be available. When ATM becomes available, however, it will play the role of a backbone network whereas MANs will be extensions of ATM in metropolitan and regional areas [55]. A single integrated voice, video, and data service using a single fabric based on IEEE MAN and BISDN protocols is a long-term goal.

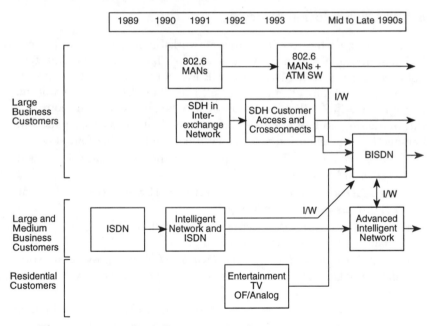

Figure 5.18   Overall communication network evolution scenario.

5.8 Conclusion

ISDN is a network that can handle all type of communication needs. The network evolution from analog to digital has been leading to the development of ISDN and BISDN. The forces for ISDN are varied. To the operating companies, it represents new information transport capabilities and new revenue opportunities. To many users, it represents a network with multimedia service capabilities. The rapid advances in related key technologies of optical fiber and microelectronics have had an impact on ISDN. Although the standards for ISDN are still evolving, the technology is well understood.

The cost of a communication network largely depends on the cost of the channels and the cost of the switches. With the rapid drop in cost of fiber optics, which offer virtually unlimited bandwidth, the cost of channels will dramatically reduce. With the advent of Gallium arsenide, warm superconductivity, and photonic switching, the cost of the switch will drop considerably [16]. The availability of ATM switches provides an ideal growth path for the MAN. The IEEE 802.6 MAN standard is compatible with ATM/BISDN and provides a natural addition to the emerging world of broadband.

Regardless of the potential problems with BISDN and its slow arrival, it is here for real, and communication engineers or users must be prepared for this eventually. Therefore, design or purchase of a MAN should be made with BISDN compatibility in mind.

References

[1] J. F. Mollenauer, "Metropolitan Area Networks and ATM Technology," *International Journal of Digital and Analog Cabled Systems*, vol. 1, no. 4, Feb. 1988, pp. 225–228.

[2] R. Rossow, "ISDN in Pacific Bell," *Proceedings of IEEE GLOBECOM*, 1990, pp. 1239–1241.

[3] W. Stallings, *Networking Standards: A Guide to OSI, ISDN, LAN, and MAN Standards*. Reading, MA:
Addison-Wesley, 1993, pp. 199–242.

[4] R. Dawes, "An Introduction to ISDN Concepts," *Elektron*, vol. 5, no. 7, July 1988, pp. 14–15.

[5] J. S. Turner, "Design of an Integrated Services Packet Network," *IEEE Journal on Selected Areas in Communications*, vol. 4, no. 8, Nov. 1986, pp. 1373–1380.

[6] A. J. Kennedy and D. C. C. Yen, "The Coming ISDN," *Information and Management*, vol. 17, no. 5, 1989, pp. 267–275.

[7] M. W. Thomas, "ISDN: Some Current Standard Difficulties," *Telecommunications Magazine*, June 1991. Also in [8], pp. 39–44.

[8] W. Stallings (ed.), *Advances in ISDN and Broadband ISDN*. Los Alamitos, CA: IEEE Computer Society Press, 1992, pp. 45–49.

[9] M. N. O. Sadiku, "Integrated Services Digital Network," in G. McClein (ed.), *Handbook of Networking and Connectivity*, in press.

[10] E. E. Summer, "ISDN: The Telephone of Tomorrow," *Radio Electronics*, Oct. 1988, pp. 41–50.

[11] J. W. Burren, "High Speed Communications — A Tutorial on the Jargon and Technologies," *Computer Networks and ISDN Systems*, vol. 23, 1991, pp. 119–124.

[12] R. T. Roca, "ISDN Architecture," *AT&T Technical Journal,* vol. 65, no. 1, 1986, pp. 5–17.

[13] K. Asatani, "CCITT Standardization of B-ISDN," *NTT Reveiw,* vol. 3, no. 3, 1991, pp. 122–133.

[14] F. C. Iffland, G. D. Norton, and J. M. Waxman, "ISDN Applications: Their Identification and Development," *IEEE Network Magazine,* Sept. 1989, pp. 6–11. Also in [8], pp. 20–25.

[15] R. W. Stephenson and S. A. McGaw, "Southwestern Bell Telephone's ISDN Experience," *IEEE Network Magazine,* Sept. 1989, pp. 25–36. Also in [8], pp. 26–33.

[16] L. Kleinrock, "ISDN — The Path to Broadband Networks," *Proceedings of the IEEE,* vol. 79, no. 2, Feb. 1991, pp. 112–117. Also in [8], pp. 151–156.

[17] S. Timms, "Broadband Communications: The Commercial Impact," *IEEE Network Magazine,* July 1989, pp. 10–15. Also in [8], pp. 157–163.

[18] M. N. Huber, "B-ISDN," in R. Dorf (ed.), *Handbook of Electrical Engineering.* Boca Raton, FL: CRC Press, 1993, pp. 1441–1447.

[19] R. Y. Awdeh, "Why Fast Packet Switching?" *IEEE Potential,* April 1993, pp. 10–12.

[20] S. E. Minzer, "Broadband ISDN and Asynchronous Transfer Mode (ATM)," *IEEE Communications,,* vol. 27, no. 9, Sept. 1989, pp. 17–24. Also in C. Dhas *et al.,* (eds.) *Broadband Switching: Architectures, Protocols, Design, and Analysis.* Los Alamitos, CA: IEEE Computer Society Press, 1991, pp. 81–89.

[21] S. Kano, K, Kitami, and M. Kawarasaki, "ISDN Standardization," *Proceedings of the IEEE,* vol. 79, no. 2, Feb. 1991, pp. 118–124.

[22] V. O. K. Li *et al.,* "A Survey of Research and Standards in High Speed Networks," *International Journal of Digital and Analog Communication Systems,* vol. 4, no. 4, 1991, pp. 269–309.

[23] M. Littlewood, "Metropolitan Area Networks and Broadband ISDN: A Perspective," *Telecommunication Journal Australia,* vol. 39, no. 2, 1989, pp. 37–44.

[24] A. Takase, J. Yanagi, and Y. Miyamori, "Broadband Subscriber Loop Systems," *Hitachi Review,* vol. 40, no. 3, 1991, pp. 199–204.

[25] W. W. Wu and Adam Livne, "ISDN: A Snapshot," *Proceedings of the IEEE,* vol. 79, no. 2, Feb. 1991, pp. 103–111. Also in [8], pp. 11–19.

[26] E. D. Sykas, K. M. Vlakos, and M. J. Hillyard, "Overview of ATM Networks: Functions and Procedures," *Computer Communications,* vol. 14, no. 10, 1991, pp. 615–626.

[27] J. Anderson, "International Standards for the Broadband ISDN User-Network Interface," *International Journal of Digital and Analog Communication Systems,* vol. 4, no. 2, 1991, pp. 143–150.

[28] R. A. Boulter, "Access to a Broadband ISDN," *British Telecom Technology Journal*, vol. 9, no. 2, 1991, pp. 20–25.

[29] B. Materna, B. J. N. Vaughan, and C. W. Britney, "Evolution from LAN and MAN Access Networks Towards the Integrated ATM Network," *Proceedings of IEEE GLOBECOM*, 1989, pp. 1455–1461.

[30] G. H. Clapp, "Broadband ISDN and Metropolitan Area Networks," *Proceedings of IEEE GLOBECOM*, 1987, pp. 2049–2054.

[31] A. Day, P. Kirton, and J. Park, "Broadband ISDN and Fast Packet Switching," *Telecommunication Journal of Australia,* vol. 39, no. 1, 1989, pp. 29–36.

[32] C. W. B. Goode, "Broadband Services and Applications," *Electrical Communications*, vol. 64, no. 2/3, 1990, pp. 124–131.

[33] I. Toda, "Migration to Broadband ISDN," *IEEE Communications Magazine*, vol. 28, no. 4, April 1990, pp. 55–58.

[34] D. J. Eigen, "Narrowband and Broadband ISDN CPE Directions," *IEEE Communications Magazine,* vol. 28, no. 4, April 1990, pp. 39–46.

[35] Anon., "ISDN—A World of Services," *Water Research News*, vol. 65, no. 1, 1991, pp. 22 26.

[36] *The Proceedings of the IEEE*, vol. 79, no. 2, Feb. 1991 is a special issue on ISDN.

[37] W. R. Byrne, A. Papanicolaou, and M. N. Ransom, "World-Wide Standardization of Broadband ISDN," *International Journal of Digital and Analog Cabled Systems,* vol. 1, 1988, pp. 181–192.

[38] I. M. Leslie, D. R. McAuley, and D. L. Tennenhouse, "ATM Everywhere?" *IEEE Network*, March 1993, pp. 40–46.

[39] G. C. Kessler, "Simplifying SONET," *LAN Magazine*, July 1991, pp. 36–46.

[40] J. J. Bae and T. Suda, "Survey of Traffic Control Schemes and Protocols in ATM Networks," *Proceedings of the IEEE*, vol. 79, no. 2, Feb. 1991, pp. 170–189.

[41] R. A. Dettra, "Metropolitan Area Networks—Data Transport Highways," *AT&T Technology*, vol. 6, no. 1, 1991, pp. 8–11.

[42] J. Lamont and M. H. Hui, "Some Experience with LAN Interconnection via Frame Relaying," *IEEE Network Magazine,* Sept. 1989, pp. 21–24,36.

[43] N. Lippis, "Frame Relay Redraws the Map for Wide-Area Networks," *Data Communications*, July 1990, pp. 80–94.

[44] J. T. Johnson, "Frame Relay: Challenging the Wide-Area Service Pictures?" *Data Communications*, Dec. 1990, pp. 56–59.

[45] M. De Prycker, "ATM Technology: A Backbone for High Speed Computer Networking," *Computer Networks and ISDN Systems,* vol. 25, 1992, pp. 357–362.

[46] C. F. Hemrich, R. W. Klessig, and J. M. McRoberts, "Switched Multi-Megabit Data Service and Early Availability via MAN Tech-

nology," *IEEE Communications Magazine*, vol. 26, no. 4, April
1988, pp. 9–14.

[47] D. M. Piscitello and M. Kramer, "Internetworking Using Switched
Multi-megabit Data Service in TCP/IP Environments," *Computer
Communication Review*, July 1990, pp. 62–71.

[48] B. Amin-Salehi, G. D. Flinchbaugh, and L. R. Pate, "Implications
of New Network Services on BISDN Capabilities," *Proceedings of
IEEE INFOCOM*, 1990, pp. 1038–1045. Also in [7], pp. 164–171.

[49] T. Cox *et al.,,* "SMDS: The Beginning of WAN Superhighways,"
Data Communications International, April 1991, pp. 105–110.

[50] J. T. Johnson, "The Many (Inter)faces of SMDS," *Data Communications*, June 1991, pp. 48–55.

[51] G. C. Kessler, "Service for Your MAN," *LAN Magazine*, Oct. 1991,
pp. 47–63.

[52] P. A. Morreale and G. M. Campbell, "Metropolitan-area Networks,"
IEEE Spectrum, May 1990, pp. 40–42.

[53] A. Ghanem, "Metropolitan Area Networks: A Corner Stone in the
Broadband Era," *Proceedings of SPIE*, vol. 1364, 1990, pp. 312–
319.

[54] W. R. Byrne *et al.*, "Evolution of Metropolitan Area Networks to
Broadband ISDN," *IEEE Communications Magazine*, Jan. 1991,
pp. 69–82.

[55] M. Gerla, L. Fratta, and J. Bannister, "Evolution of LANs and
MANs Towards High Speeds: Gigabits per Second and Beyond,"
*European Transactions on Telecommunications and Related Tech-
nologies,* vol. 2, no. 1, 1991, pp. 89–104.

Glossary and Acronyms

ANSI   American National Standards Institute.

Application Layer   This is layer 7 (highest layer) in the OSI protocol hierarchy. It provides an interface between user programs and data communication.

ASCII   American Standard Code for Information Interchange.

Asynchronous Transmission   Transmission without clocking or one with characters containing their own timing information so that no separate clock is required.

Asynchronous Transfer Mode (ATM)   A packetized multiplexing scheme that allows services of difference bit rates to be efficiently carried on an optical fiber; the broadband ISDN mode similar to asynchronous time-division multiplexing.

Attenuation   Reduction in magnitude of the current, voltage, or power of a signal.

Backbone   A network that links two or more other local networks.

Bandwidth   The range of frequencies that are passed by a communications channel without significant attenuation.

Baseband   A method of transmitting signals without modulation.

BISDN   Broadband Integrated Services Digital Network; standards being developed for ISDN to handle services such as video that require high bandwidth.

Bit   Abbreviation for binary digit.

Bit Rate   Number of bits per second transmitted or received.

BIU   Bus Interface Unit; the device that physically connects the data equipment to the LAN.

Bridge   A device for interconnecting LANs that operates at the data link layer.

Broadband   Communication links that can support two or more channels that carry signals simultaneously; also regarded as a technology that uses frequency-division multiplexing over a single communication medium to provide multiple physical channels.

Broadcast   Simultaneous transmission of signal to a number of nodes.

Brouter   A device for interconnecting LANs that routes packets using network layer protocols and bridges traffic at the data link layer.

Byte   Eight bits of information; also called an *octet*.

CATV   Community Antenna TeleVision; a communications service that provides TV signals to large community through cable.

CCITT   Consultative Committee on International Telegraphy and Telephony; an international body that develops telecommunications standards.

Circuit Switching   A switching mechanism that establishes a dedicated path between users held for the duration of the communication. Most telephone connections are circuit switched.

Coaxial Cable   A transmission medium consisting of an insulated core surrounded by a braided shield.

Concentrator   A central device to which other devices are connected.

Connection-Oriented Transmission   Data transmission involving setting up a connection before transmission and disconnection after all data has been transmitted; analogous to a telephone call.

Connectionless Service   Treats each packet or datagram as a separate entity that contains the source and destination addresses. Connectionless services can drop packets or deliver them out of sequence.

Connectionless Transmission   Data transmission without setting up a connection; analogous to posting a letter.

Crosstalk   Unwanted transfer of energy from one circuit to another.

CSMA   Carrier Sense Multiple Access. A medium mechanism used in LANs.

CSMA/CD   Carrier Sense Multiple Access with Collision Detection; CSMA with sensing during transmission to detect collisions.

Data Link Layer   Layer 2 of the OSI reference model.

Delay   See *Transfer Delay*.

Downstream This term refers to a node or station immediately next to the reference one in the transmission path.

DQDB Distributed-Queue Dual Bus; the IEEE 802.6 standard MAN.

Electronic Mail A means of exchanging mail-like messages over a communication network.

EMI ElectroMagnetic Interference caused by a conductor.

Ethernet A bus based LAN using CSMA/CD medium access protocol.

Fairness Equitable treatment of all users, especially in terms of access to a network.

FCC Federal Communications Commission; a regulatory authority for telecommunications in the US.

FDDI Fiber Distributed Data Interface; a high-speed (100 Mbps), token passing LAN using fiber-optics links.

Fiber Optics Through thin filament of glass transmission of a signal-encoded light beam by means of total internal reflection.

Flow Control A means by which a receiving entity limits the amount of data sent by the transmitting entity.

Fragmentation A process through which a data frame is broken into smaller frames.

Frame The basic unit of transmission within a network.

Frame Relay An ISDN service that provides unacknowledged transfer of frames between users.

Gateway A device for interconnecting dissimilar LANs or systems when some high-level protocol conversion is required.

Header Control information that precedes user data.

IEEE The Institute of Electrical and Electronics Engineers.

IEEE 802 The committee assigned by IEEE to provide standards for LANs.

IEEE 802.2 IEEE standard for logical link control protocols.

IEEE 802.3 IEEE standard for CSMA/CD protocols.

IEEE 802.4 IEEE standard for token bus MAC protocols.

IEEE 802.5 IEEE standard for token ring MAC protocols.

IEEE 802.6 IEEE standard for metropolitan area networks.

ISDN Integrated Services Digital Network; an end-to-end digital network that supports a wide range of services accessed by a limited set of multipurpose user-network interfaces.

ISO International Standards Organization; an international body responsible for setting standards.

Isochronous Service One in which a bit stream is sent at fixed, periodic intervals. Nonisochronous services include voice and file transfer.

LAN   Local Area Network; a network that interconnects telecommunications devices in a limited geographical area such as a building or campus.

Layer   A conceptual region that embodies some functions between an upper logical boundary and a lower logical boundary.

LLC   Logical Link Control; the upper part of the data link layer.

MAC   Medium Access Control; a mechanism that ensures that only one node has access to the medium at a time.

Mail Server   A computer system that provides an electronic mail service.

MAN   Metropolitan Area Network; a network that links a number of telecommunications devices within a large metropolitan area.

Microwave   An electromagnetic wave in the frequency range of 3 to 30 GHz.

Modem   A modulator/demodulator that converts a digital bit stream into an analog signal (modulation) and vice versa (demodulation).

Multiplexing   A process of combining separate communication channels into one composite channel.

Multiport Bridge   A bridge that connects three or more networks.

Network Layer   Layer 3 of the OSI reference model.

Node   A station or data communication equipment at a geographical location in a telecommunication network.

Nonreturn to Zero (NRZ)   A signaling scheme in which a high-priority signal represents 1 and a low-priority signal represents 0.

Nonreturn to Zero Invert on Ones (NRZI)   A signaling scheme in which a polarity transition at the beginning of the bit time is used to represent a 1 and the absence of a transition represents a 0.

Octet   See *Byte*.

Optical Fiber   Communication medium used for fiber optics.

OSI   Open Systems Interconnection; a model architecture and protocol hierarchy set by ISO.

Packet   A group of bits of information sent across a communication network.

Packet Switching   A switching mechanism that involves breaking a message into packets, which are routed independently of one another to their destination in a store-and-forward manner over multiple virtual circuits.

PBX   Private Branch Exchange; a telephone exchange on the user's premises.

Physical Layer   Layer 1 of the OSI reference model.

Presentation Layer   Layer 6 of the OSI reference model.

Propagation Time Time interval between a signal's transmission at the sending node and its reception at the receiving node.

Protocol A formal set of rules for exchanging of information between nodes.

Random Access An uncontrolled access to a transmission medium in which stations transmit when ready and later resolve any conflict that may arise.

Repeater A physical layer device for amplifying or regenerating signals.

Router A network layer device that routes data between LANs.

Routing Technique for transmitting a message from source to destination.

Session Layer Layer 5 of the OSI reference model.

Server A LAN-connected computer sharing its resources (hard disks, CD-ROM drives, printers, E-mail, modems, etc.) with other LAN-connected computers.

Signaling The procedure for creating and clearing connections.

Slot A unit of transmission on the bus.

SONET Synchronous Optical NETwork; a standard for a metropolitan area network using optical fiber technology.

Synchronous Traffic Occurring regularly in relatively predictable quantities.

Synchronous Transfer Mode (STM) A transmission scheme that assigns time slots for channels on a fixed, regular basis.

Terminal A collection of hardware and possibly software that provides a direct user interface to a network.

Throughput Rate at which data is transmitted across a network.

Token A special frame that allows a node to transmit data.

Topology Arrangement of nodes in a network or the shape of the network (e.g., ring, bus, star, etc.)

Transfer Delay The time between the arrival of a packet to a node interface and its complete delivery at the destination node.

Transport Layer Layer 4 of the OSI reference model.

Twisted Pair A communication medium consisting of two copper wires that are twisted to minimize interference.

Virtual Channel A logical connection between two users.

Virtual Circuit A path between two nodes established at the beginning of transmission by a packet-switching mechanism.

WAN Wide Area Network; a network spanning a large geographical area, possibly the entire globe.

Selected Bibliography

Due to space limitations, only journal articles and books are included in this bibliography. Relevant conference articles can be found in the reference section of each chapter.

A. MANs IN GENERAL

B. W. Abeysundara and A. E. Kamal, "High-Speed Local Area Networks and Their Performance: A Survey," *ACM Computing Surveys,* vol. 23, no. 2, June 1991, pp. 221–264.

E. Ball *et al.,* "Local Area Network Bridges," *Computer Communications*, vol. 11, no. 3, June 1988, pp. 115–118.

N. L. Ball and R. T. P. Kummer, "A Bridge Protocol for Creating a Spanning Tree Topology within an IEEE 802 Extended LAN Environment," *Computer Networks and ISDN Systems*, vol. 13, 1987, pp. 323–332.

J. A. Bannister, L. Fratta, and M. Gerla, "Designing Metropolitan Area Networks for High-Performance Applications," *Computer Networks and ISDN Systems*, 1990, pp. 223–230.

W. Bauerfeld, "A Tutorial on Network Gateways and Interworking of LANs and WANs," *Computer Networks and ISDN Systems*, vol. 13, 1987, pp. 187–193.

B. Berg and R. H. Deng, "End-to-End Performance of Interconnected LANs," *Computer Communications*, vol. 14, no. 2, March 1991, pp. 105–112.

J. A. Berntsen, *et al.*, "MAC Layer Interconnection of IEEE 802 Local Area Networks," *Computer Networks and ISDN Systems*, vol. 10, no. 5, 1985, pp. 259–273.

D. Bertsekas and R. Gallager, *Data Networks.* Englewood Cliffs, NJ: Prentice-Hall, 1992.

E. W. Biersack, "Annotated Bibliography on Network Interconnection," *IEEE Journal Selected Areas in Communications*, vol. 8, no. 1, Jan. 1990, pp. 22–41.

J. Birch, L. G. Christensen, and M. Skov, "A Programmable 800 Mbit/s CRC Check/Generator Unit for LANs and MANs," *Computer Networks and ISDN Systems*, vol. 24, 1992, pp. 109–118.

A. Bondavalli, M. Conti, E. Gregori, L. Nenzini, and L. Strigini, "MAC Protocols for High-Speed MANs: Performance Comparisons for a Family of Fasnet-Based Protocols," *Computer Networks and ISDN Systems*, vol. 18, 1989/90, pp. 97–113.

F. Borgonovo, "ExpressMAN: Exploiting Traffic Locality in Expressnet," *IEEE Journal on Selected Areas in Communications,* vol. SAC-5, no. 9, Dec. 1987, pp. 1436–1443.

J. W. Burren, "High Speed Communications—A Tutorial on the Jargon and Technologies," *Computer Networks and ISDN Systems*, vol. 23, 1991, pp. 119–124.

W. Bux and D. Gillo, "Flow Control in Local Area Networks of Interconnected Token Rings," *IEEE Transactions on Communications*, vol. 33, no. 10, October 1985, pp. 1058–1066.

Y. C. Cheng and T. G. Robertazzi, "Annotated Bibliography of Local Communication System Interconnection," *IEEE Journal Selected Areas in Communications*, vol. 5, no. 9, Dec. 1987, pp. 1492–1499.

R. Cole, "A Method for Interconnecting Heterogeneous Computer Networks," *Software Practice and Experience*, vol. 17, no. 6, June 1987, pp. 387–397.

M. Coronaro, G. Freschi, M. Iudica, C. Pavanelli, and D. Roffinella, "Metropolitan Area Networks. Standards, Services and Performance," *European Transactions on Telecommunication and Related Technologies*, vol. 2, no. 2, Mar.–Apr. 1991, pp. 189–198.

R. E. Dettra, "Metropolitan Area Networks—Data Transport Highways," *AT&T Technology,* vol. 6, no. 1, 1991, pp. 8–11.

R. C. Dixon and D. A. Pitt, "Addressing, Bridging, and Source Routing," *IEEE Network*, vol. 2, no. 1, Jan. 1988, pp. 25–32.

C. Ersoy and S. S. Panwar, "Topological Design of Interconnected LAN/MAN Networks," *IEEE Journal on Selected Areas in Communications,* vol. 11, no. 8, Oct. 1993, pp. 1172–1182.

G. M. Exley and L. F. Merakos, "Throughput-Delay Performance of Interconnected CSMA Local Area Networks," *IEEE Journal on Selected Areas in Communications*, vol. 5, no. 9, Dec. 1987, pp. 1380–1390.

R, M. Falconer and L. Adams, "Orwell: A Protocol for an Integrated Services Local Network," *British Telecommunication Technical Journal,* vol. 3, no. 4, October 1985, pp. 27–28.

F. Fluckiger, "Gateways and Converters in Computer Networks," *Computer Networks and ISDN Systems*, vol. 16, 1988/89, pp. 55–59.

J. Gantz, "Does the World Need MANs?" *Networking Management*, vol. 8, no. 6, 1990, pp. 70–72.

M. Gerla and L. Fratta, "Tree Structured Fiber Optics MAN's," *IEEE Journal on Selected Areas in Communications,* vol. SAC-6, no. 6, July 1988, pp. 934–943.

M. Gerla, L. Fratta, and J. Bannister, "Evolution of LANs and MANs Towards High Speeds: Gigabits per Second and Beyond," *European Transactions on Telecommunication and Related Technologies,* vol. 2, no 1, 1991, pp. 89–104.

M. Gerla and L. Kleinrock, "Congestion Control in Interconnected LANs," *IEEE Network*, vol. 2, no. 1, Jan. 1988, pp. 72–76.

P. E. Green (ed.), *Network Interconnection and Protocol Conversion.* New York: IEEE Press, 1988.

H. S. Hassanein and A. E. Kamal, "Study of the Behaviour of Hubnet," *IEEE Proceedings* Pt. E. vol. 140, no. 2, Mar. 1993, pp. 134–144.

J. Heinanen, "Review of Backbone Technologies," *Computer Networks and ISDN Systems*, vol. 21, 1991, pp. 229–245.

C. F. Hemrick, R. W. Klessig, and J. M. McRoberts, "Switched Multi-Megabit Data Service and Early Availability via MAN Technology," *IEEE Communications Magazine*, vol. 26, no. 4, April 1988, pp. 9–14.

J. Houldsworth, M. Taylor, K. Caves, A. Flatman, and K. Crook, *Open System LANs and their Global Interconnection.* Oxford: Butterworth-Heinemann, 1991, pp. 10.22–10.36.

O. C. Ibe and X. Cheng, "Analysis of Interconnected Systems of Token Ring Networks," *Computer Communications*, vol. 13, no. 3, 1990, pp. 136–142.

——, "Approximate Analysis of Asymmetric Single-Service Token-Passing Systems," *IEEE Transactions on Communications*, vol. 37, no. 6, June 1989, pp. 572–577.

O. C. Ibe and R. C. Howe, "Architectures for Metropolitan Area Networks," *Computer Communications*, vol. 12, no. 6, Dec. 1989, pp. 315–323.

——, "An Integrated CATV-Type Metropolitan Area Network," *Computer Networks and ISDN Systems*, vol. 13, 1987, pp. 291–299.

H. Inose (ed.), *Telecommunication Technologies*. Amsterdam: North-Holland, 1983.

J. Janecek, S. Jedlik, and M. Meloun, "Effectiveness of Bridging in Multiprotocol LANs," *Microprocessing and Microprogramming*, vol. 37, 1993, pp. 205–208.

T. Kaneko, S. Hosokawa, and K. Yamashita, "An Interconnection Method of Two CSMA/CD LANs," *Memoirs of the Faculty of Engineering, Osaka City University*, vol. 29, 1988, pp. 81–89.

A. I. Karshmer and J. N. Thomas, "Computer Networking on Cable TV Plants," *IEEE Network*, vol. 6, no. 6, Nov. 1992, pp. 32–40.

A. I. Karshmer, J. N. Thomas, and J. M. Phelan, "TVNet II: A Cable TV Based Metropolitan Area Networks Using the KEDS Protocol," *Microprocessing and Microprogramming*, vol. 30, no. 1-5, 1990, pp. 627–636.

A. I. Karshmer and R. Yan, "A CATV Based Metropolitan Area Networks Using Distributed Switching," *Microprocessing and Microprogramming*, vol. 37, 1993, pp. 197–200.

G. C. Kessler and D. A. Train, *Metropolitan Area Networks: Concepts, Standards, and Services*. New York: McGraw-Hill, 1992.

B. G. Kim (ed.), *Current Advances in LANs, MANs, and ISDN*. Norwood, MA: Artech House, 1989.

R. W. Klessig, "Overview of Metropolitan Area Networks," *IEEE Communications Magazine*, vol. 24, no. 1, Jan. 1986, pp. 9–15.

R. Krishnan and N. F. Maxemchuk, "Life Beyond Linear Topologies," *IEEE Network*, vol. 7, no. 2, Mar. 1993, pp. 48–54.

R. Kuruppillai and N. Bengtson, "Performance Analysis in Local Area Networks of Interconnected Token Rings," *Computer Communications*, vol. 11, no. 2, April 1988, pp. 59–64.

A. A. Lazar, G. Pacifici, and J. S. White, "Real-Time Traffic Measurements on MAGNET II," *IEEE Journal on Selected Areas in Communications*, vol. 8, no. 3, April 1990, pp. 467–483.

A. A. Lazar, A. Patir, T. Takahashi, and M. El Zarki, "MAGNET: Columbia's Integrated Network Testbed," *IEEE Journal on Selected Areas in Communications*, vol. SAC-3, no. 6, Nov. 1985, pp. 859–871.

A. A. Lazar, A. T. Temple, and R. Gidron, "MAGNET II: A Metropolitan Area Network Based on Asynchronous Time Sharing," *IEEE Journal on Selected Areas in Communications*, vol. 8, no. 8, Oct. 1990, pp. 1582–1594.

A. A. Lazar and J. S. White, "Packetized Video on MAGNET," *Optical Engineering*, vol. 26, no. 7, July 1987, pp. 596–602.

V. O. K. Li, J. F. Chang, K. C. Lee, and T. S. Yang, "A Survey of Research and Standards in High-Speed Networks," *International Journal of Digital and Analog Communications System*, vol. 4, no. 4, 1991, pp. 269- -309.

J. O. Limb, "Load-Controlled Scheduling of Traffic on High-Speed Metropolitan Area Networks," *IEEE Transactions on Communications*, vol. 37, no. 11, Nov. 1989, pp. 1144–1150.

J. O. Limb and L. E. Flamm, "A Distributed Local Area Network Packet Protocol for Combined Voice and Data Transmission," *IEEE Journal on Selected Areas in Communications*, vol. SAC-1, no. 5, Nov. 1983, pp. 926–934.

J. O. Limb and C. Flores, "Description of Fasnet—A Unidirectional Local-Area Communication Network," *Bell System Technical Journal*, vol. 61, no. 7, Sept. 1982, pp. 1413–1440.

N. F. Maxemchuk, "Regular Mesh Topologies in Local and Metropolitan Area Networks," *AT & T Technical Journal*, vol. 64, no. 7, Sept. 1985, pp. 1659–1685.

——, "Routing in the Manhattan Street Network," *IEEE Transactions on Communications*, vol. 35, no. 5, May 1987, pp. 503–512.

M. Miyazawa, K. Kinoshita, and K. Unemoto, "Standardization Activities on Private Networks," *NTT Review*, vol. 5, no. 2, March 1993, 113–118.

J. F. Mollenauer, "Standards for Metropolitan Area Networks," *IEEE Communications Magazine*, vol. 26, no. 4, 1988, pp. 15–19.

——, "Networking for Greater Metropolitan Areas," *Data Communications International*, Feb. 1988, pp. 115–128.

——, "Metropolitan Area Networks: A New Application for Fiber," *Photonics Spectra*, vol. 24, no. 3, 1990, pp. 159–161.

P. A. Morreale and G. M. Campbell, "Metropolitan-Area Networks," *IEEE Spectrum*, May 1990, pp. 40- -42.

M. Murata and H. Takagi, "Performance of Token Ring Networks with a Finite Capacity Bridge," *Computer Networks and ISDN Systems*, vol. 24, 1992, pp. 45–64.

C. Panasuk, "Designer's Reference," *Electronic Design*, Dec. 27, 1984, pp. 87–94.

A. Patir, T. Takashashi, Y. Tamura, M. El Zarki, and A. A. Lazar, "An Optical Fiber-Based Integrated LAN for MAGNET's Testbed Environment," *IEEE Journal on Selected Areas in Communications,* vol. SAC-3, no. 6, Nov. 1985, pp. 872–881.

A. Pattavina, "Performance Evaluation of ATM Switches with Input and Output Queuing," *International Journal of Digital and Analog Cabled Systems*, vol. 3, no. 3, 1990, pp. 227–286.

R. Perlman, A. Harvey, and G. Varghese, "Choosing the Appropriate ISO Layer for LAN Interconnection," *IEEE Network*, vol. 2, no.1, Jan. 1988, pp. 81–86.

R. L. Pickholtz, *Local Area and Multiple Access Networks.* Rockville, MD: Computer Science Press, 1986.

G. S. Poo, "Performance Measurement of Interconnected CSMA/ CD LANs," *Computer Communications*, vol. 12, no. 1, Feb. 1989, pp. 3–9.

G. Pujolle (ed.), *High-Capacity Local and Metropolitan Area Networks.* Berlin: Springer-Verlag, 1990.

R. Reardon, *Networks for the 1990s.* New York: John Wiley & Sons, 1988.

T. G. Robertazzi, "Toroidal Networks," *IEEE Communications Magazine*, vol. 26, no. 6, June 1988, pp. 45–50.

M. A. Rodrigues, "Evaluating Performance of High-Speed Multiaccess Networks," *IEEE Network Magazine*, vol. 4, no. 2, May 1990, pp. 36–41.

I. Rubin and J. K. Lee, "Performance Analysis of Interconnected Metropolitan Area Circuit-Switched Telecommunications Networks," *IEEE Transactions on Communications*, vol. 36, no. 2, Feb. 1988, pp. 171–185.

I. Rubin and Z. Tsai, "Performance of Double-Tier Access-Control Schemes Using a Polling Backbone for Metropolitan and Interconnected Communication Networks," *IEEE Journal of Selected Areas in Communications*, vol. SAC-5, no. 9, Nov. 1987, pp. 1403–1417.

M. N. O. Sadiku, "Metropolitan Area Networks," in G. McClein (ed.), *Handbook of Networking and Connectivity*, in press.

H. Salwen, R. Boule, and J. N. Chiappa, "Examination of the Applicability of Router and Bridging Techniques," *IEEE Network*, vol. 2, no. 1, Jan. 1988, pp. 77–80.

W. M. Seifert, "Bridges and Routers," *IEEE Network*, vol. 2, no. 1, Jan. 1988, pp. 57–64.

M. Skov, "Implementation of Physical and Media Access Protocols for High-Speed Networks," *IEEE Communications Magazine*, June 1989, pp. 45–53.

J. P. Slone and A. Drinan (eds.), *Local Area Networks*. Boston, MA: Auerbach Publishers, 1991.

M. Sveda, "Small Area Network Interconnection," *Microprocessing and Microprogramming*, vol. 37, no. 1–5, Jan. 1993, pp. 193–196.

W. Stallings, *Network Standards: A Guide to OSI, ISDN, LAN, and MAN Standards*. Reading, MA: Addison-Wesley, 1993.

——, *Local and Metropolitan Area Networks*. New York: Macmillan, 4th ed., 1993.

I. Stavrakakis and D. Kazakos, "Performance Analysis of a Star Topology of Interconnected Networks Under 2nd-Order Markov Network Output Processes," *IEEE Transactions on Communications*, vol. 38, no. 10, Oct. 1990, pp. 1724–1731.

D. T. W. Sze, "A Metropolitan Area Network," *IEEE Journal on Selected Areas in Communications*, vol. SAC-3, no. 6, 1985, pp. 815–824.

A. S. Tanenbaum, *Computer Networks*. Englewood Cliffs, NJ: Prentice-Hall, 1981.

F. A. Tobagi, F. Borgonovo, and L. Fratta, "Expressnet: A High-Performance Integrated-Service Local Area Network," *IEEE Journal on Selected Areas in Communications*, vol. SAC-1, no. 5, Nov. 1983, pp. 898–913.

C. W. Tseng and B. U. Chen, "D-Net: A New Scheme for High Data Rate Optical Local Area Networks," *IEEE Journal on Selected Areas in Communications,* vol. SAC-1, no. 3, April 1983, pp. 493–499.

F. Vakil, M. T. Hsiao, and A. A. Lazar, "Flow Control in Integrated Local Area Networks," *Performance Evaluation,* vol. 7, 1987, pp. 43–57.

J. S. K. Wong and Y. Kang, "Distributed and Fail-Safe Routing Algorithms in Toroidal-Based Metropolitan Area Networks," *Computer Networks and ISDN Systems,* vol. 18, 1989/90, pp. 379–391.

B. FDDI

W. E. Burr, "The FDDI Data Optical Link," *IEEE Communications Magazine,* vol. 24, no. 5, May 1986, pp. 8–23.

D. Dykeman and W. Bux, "Analysis and Tuning of the FDDI Media Access Control Protocol," *IEEE Journal on Selected Areas in Communications,* vol. 6, no. 6, July 1988, pp. 997–1010.

R. L. Fink and F. Ross, "FFOL—An FDDI Follow-On LAN," *Computer Communication Review,* vol. 21, no. 2, April 1991, pp. 15–16.

B. F. Gearing, "Building Wiring Standards and their Impact on FDDI," *Fiber Optics Magazine,* Sept. 1992, pp. 13–18.

E. Gronert, "Public FDDI Today, MANs Tomorrow," *Data Communications International,* Nov. 1990, pp. 49–51.

V. Iyer and S. Joshi, "FDDI's 100M-bps Protocol Improves on 802.5 Spec's 4M-bps Limit," *EDN,* May 2, 1985, pp. 151–156, 158, 160.

A. P. Jayasumana and P. N. Werahera, "Performance of Fibre Distributed Data Interface Network for Multiple Classes of Traffic," *IEEE Proceedings,* Pt. E, vol. 137, no. 5, Sept. 1990, pp. 401–408.

M. J. Johnson, "Proof that Timing Requirements of the FDDI Token Ring Protocol are Satisfied," *IEEE Transactions on Communications,* vol. 35, no. 6, June 1987, pp. 620–625.

S. P. Joshi, "High-Performance Networks: A Focus on the Fiber Distributed Data Interface (FDDI) Standard," *IEEE Micro,* vol. 6, no. 3, June 1986, pp. 8–14.

D. A. Krohn, "Twisted Wire Pair Versus Optical Fibers for FDDI," *Fiber Optics Magazine,* Sept. 1992, pp. 25–28.

R. O. LaMaire, "An M/G/1 Vacation Model of an FDDI Station," *IEEE Journal on Selected Areas in Communications,* vol. 9, no. 2, Feb. 1991, pp. 257–265.

L. Mantelman, "Incompatible Bridges Stymie Use of FDDI as LAN Backbone," *Data Communications International*, Sept. 1989, pp. 39–44.

J. F. McCool, "FDDI: Getting to Know the Inside of the Ring," *Data Communication Magazine*, vol. 17, no. 3, March 1988, pp. 185–192.

S. Mirchandani and R. Khanna (eds.), *FDDI: Technology and Applications*. New York: John Wiley & Sons, 1993.

W. M. Price, "MAN Provides FDDI to Tallahassee," *Telephony*, Feb. 15, 1993, pp. 16–17.

W. M. Price and J. F. Westmark, "Tallahassee's CMDS: The First FDDI MAN," *Business Communications Review*, vol. 21, no. 10, Oct. 1991, pp. 37–41.

M. Rose *et al.*, "Migrating to FDDI on Your Next Big LAN Installation," *Data Communications International*, June 21, 1989, pp. 35–43.

F. E. Ross, "FDDI—A Tutorial," *IEEE Communications Magazine*, vol. 24, no. 5, May 1986, pp. 10–17.

———, "An Overview of FDDI: The Fiber Distributed Data Interface," *IEEE Journal on Selected Areas in Communications*, vol. SAC-7, no. 7, Sept. 1989, pp. 1043–1051.

F. E. Ross and R. L. Fink, "Overview of FFOL—FDDI Follow-On LAN," *Computer Communications*, vol. 15, no. 1, Jan./Feb. 1992, pp. 5–10.

F. E. Ross and J. R. Hamstra, "Forging FDDI," *IEEE Journal on Selected Areas in Communications*, vol. 11, no. 2, Feb. 1993, pp. 181–190.

F. E. Ross, J. R. Hamstra, and R. L. Fink, "FDDI—A LAN Among MANs," *Computer Communication Review*, vol. 20, no. 3, July 1990, pp. 16–31

K. C. Sevick and M. J. Johnson, "Cycle Time Properties of the FDDI Token Ring Protocol," *IEEE Transactions on Software Engineering,*, vol. 13, no. 3, 1987, pp. 376–385.

P. D. Stigall and C. D. Biagioli, "SONET Utilization from FDDI Sources," *Computer and Electrical Engineering*, vol. 18, no. 5, 1992, pp. 373–388.

M. Tangemann and K. Sauer, "Performance Analysis of the Timed Token Protocol of FDDI and FDDI-II," *IEEE Journal on Selected Areas in Communications*, vol. 9, no. 2, Feb. 1991, pp. 271–278.

M. Taylor, "FDDI—The High Speed Network for the Nineties," *ICL Technical Journal,* vol. 8, no. 2, Nov. 1992, pp. 225–241.

K. J. Thurber, "Getting a Handle on FDDI," *Data Communications International,* June 21, 1989, pp. 28- -32.

D. Tsao, "FDDI: Chapter Two," *Data Communications,* Dec. 21, 1991, pp. 59–70.

D. Wallace, "Will ATM Sink FDDI?" *Communications International,* vol. 19, no. 10, Oct. 1992, pp. 77- -78.

G. Watson and D. Cunningham, "FDDI and Beyond: A Network for the 90s," *IEEE Review,* April 1990, pp. 131–134.

C. DQDB

S. Banerjee and B. Mukherjee, "Incorporating Continuation-of-Message Information, Slot Reuse, and Fairness in DQDB Networks," *Computer Networks and ISDN Systems,* vol. 24, no. 2, April 1992, pp. 153–169.

C. Bisdikian, "Waiting Time Analysis in a Single Buffer DQDB (802.6) network," *IEEE Journal on Selected Areas in Communications,* vol. 8, no. 8, Oct. 1990, pp. 1565–1573.

——, "A Performance Analysis of the IEEE 802.6 (DQDB) Subnetwork with the Bandwidth Balancing Mechanism," *Computer Networks and ISDN Systems,* vol. 24, no. 5, June 1992, pp. 367–385.

M. Bonatti (ed.), *Teletraffic Science for New Cost-Effective Systems, Networks, and Services.* Amsterdam: North-Holland, 1989.

F. Borgonovo, A. Lombardo, and D. Panno, "FQDB: A Fair Multi-segment MAC Protocol for Dual Bus Networks," *IEEE Journal on Selected Areas in Communications,* vol. 11, no. 8, Oct. 1993, pp. 1240–1248.

R. Brandwein, T. Cox, and J. Dahl, "IEEE 802.6 Physical Layer Convergence Procedures," *IEEE LCS Magazine,* vol. 1, no. 2, May 1990, pp. 26–30.

S. Casale, V. Catania, A. La Corte, and L. Vita, "Service Management on an ATM DQDB MAN," *Computer Communications,* vol. 16, no. 3, May 1992, pp. 147–154.

M. Conti, E. Gregori and L. Lenzini, "On the Approximation of the Slot Occupancy Pattern in a DQDB Network," *Performance Evaluation,* vol. 16, no. 1–3, Nov. 1992, pp. 129–158.

——, "A Methodological Approach to an Extensive Analysis of DQDB Performance and Fairness," *IEEE Journal on Selected Areas in Communications*, vol. 9, no. 1, Jan. 1991, pp. 76–87.

——, "A Comprehensive Analysis of DQDB," *European Transactions on Telecommunication and Related Technologies*, vol. 2, no. 4, Jul./Aug. 1991, pp. 403–413.

S. Covaci, "Distributed Management Process for Queued Arbitrated Traffic in a DQDB MAN," *Computer Communications*, vol. 16, no. 1, Jan. 1993, pp. 13–18.

A. Fenyves, and A. Lazzari, "Operational Experience with DQDB MANs," *Computer Communications*, vol. 16, no. 1, Jan. 1993, pp. 19–26.

M. Gagnaire, J. M. Canet, and P. Godlewski, "An Investigation of Packetized Voice on the DQDB Network," *Computer Communications Review*, vol. 22, no. 4, Oct. 1992, pp. 79–84.

M. W. Garrett and S. Q. Li, "A Study of Slot Reuse in Dual Bus Multiple Access Networks," *IEEE Journal of Selected Areas in Communications*, Feb. 1991, pp. 248–256.

E. L. Hahne, A. K. Choudhury, and N. F. Maxemchuk, "DQDB Networks with and Without Bandwidth Balancing," *IEEE Transactions on Communication*, vol. 40, no. 7, July 1992, pp. 1192–1204.

G. Horn, "Isochronous Services on DQDB Metropolitan Area Networks," *IFIP Transactions C, Communications Systems*, Jan. 1992, pp. 65–76.

A. Ippoliti, A. Albanese, P. Coppo, D. Ercole, and M. Ullio, "Internetworking of Bearer Services on ATM and IEEE 802.6 Networks," *CSELT Technical Reports*, vol. 20, no. 5, Oct. 1992, pp. 381–385.

M. J. Karol and R. D. Gitlin, "High Performance Optical Local and Metropolitan Area Networks: Enhancements of FDDI and IEEE 802.6 DQDB," *IEEE Journal in Selected Areas in Communications*, vol. 8, no. 8, Oct. 1990, pp. 1439–1448.

Q. Y. Lee, H. Sirisena, K. Pawlikowski, and W. Kennedy, "Fairness Improvement Using Multiple-Slot Reservation on DQDB," *Computer Communications Review*, vol. 22, no. 4, Oct. 1992, pp. 79–84.

J. Liebeherr., I. F. Akyildiz, and A. N. Tantawi, "An Effective Scheme for Pre-Emptive Priorities in Dual Bus Metropolitan Area Networks," *Computer Communications Review*, vol. 22, no. 4, Oct. 1992, pp. 161- -169.

N. F. Maxemchuk and R. Krishnan, "A Comparison of Linear and Mesh Topologies—DQDB and the Manhattan Street Network," *IEEE Journal in Selected Areas in Communications*, vol. 11, no. 8, Oct. 1993, pp. 1278–1289.

B. Mukherjee and S. Banerjee, "Alternative Strategies for Improving the Fairness in and an Analytical Model of DQDB Networks," *IEEE Transactions on Computers*, vol. 43, no. 3, Feb. 1993, pp. 151–167.

B. Mukherjee and C. Bisdikian, "A Journey Through the DQDB Network Literature," *Performance Evaluation*, pp. 129–158.

A. Myles, "DQDB Simulation and MAC Protocol Analysis," *Electronics Letters*, vol. 25, no. 9, Apr. 27, 1989, pp. 616–618.

R. M. Newman, Z. L. Budrikis, and J. L. Hullett, "The QPSX Man," *IEEE Communications Magazine*, April 1988, vol. 26, no. 4, pp. 20–28.

A. R. Pach, S. Palazzo, and D. Panno, "Slot Pre-Using in IEEE 802.6 Metropolican Area Networks," *IEEE Journal in Selected Areas in Communications*, vol. 11, no. 8, Oct. 1993, pp. 1249–1258.

V. P. T. Phung and R. Breault, "On the Unpredictable Behavior of DQDB," *Computer Networks and ISDN Systems*, vol. 24, no. 2, April 1992, pp. 145–152.

P. G. Potter and M. Zukerman, "A Discrete Shared Processor Model for DQDB," *Computer Networks and ISDN Systems*, vol. 20, no. 1–5, Dec. 1990, pp. 217–222.

———, "Analysis of a Discrete Multi-Priority Queuing System Involving a Central Shared Processor Serving Many Queues," *IEEE Journal of Selected Areas in Communications*, vol. 9, no. 2, Feb. 1991, pp. 194–202.

X. Qian, S. Wakid, D. Vaman, and D. Cypher, "Architectures for BISDN Networks: a Performance Study," *International Journal of Satellite Communications*, vol. 9, no. 5, 1991, pp. 313–327.

M. A. Rodrigues, "Evaluating Performance of High-Speed Multiaccess Networks," *IEEE Network Magazine*, vol. 4, no. 2, May 1990, pp. 36–41.

M. N. O. Sadiku and A. S. Arvind, "Annotated Bibliography on DQDB", *Computer Communication Review*, vol. 24, no. 1, Jan. 1994, pp. 21–36.

K. Sauer and W. Schodl, "Performance Aspects of the DQDB Protocol," *Computer Networks and ISDN Systems*, vol. 20, no. 1–5, Dec. 1990, pp. 253–260.

——, "Approximate Performance Analysis of the DQDB Access Protocol," *Computer Networks and ISDN Systems*, vol. 20, no. 1–5, Dec. 1990, pp. 231–240.

O. Sharon and A. Segall, "A Simple Scheme for Slot Reuse Without Latency for a Dual Bus Configuration," *IEEE/ACM Transactions on Networking*, vol. 1, no. 1, Feb. 1993, pp. 96–104.

M. T. Yap and D. Hutchison, "An Emulator for Evaluating DQDB Performance," *Computer Networks and ISDN Systems*, vol. 25, no. 11, June 1993, pp. 1177–1204.

T. Yokotani, H. Sato, S. Nakatsuka, and T. Shikama, "The New Slot Reutilization Scheme in DQDB MAN," *IEICE Transactions*, vol. E74, no. 9, Sept. 1991, pp. 2728–2736.

M. Zukerman and P. G. Potter, "The Effect of Eliminating the Standby State on DQDB Performance Under Overload," *International Journal of Digital and Analog Cabled Systems*, vol. 2, no. 3, Jul./Sept. 1989, pp. 179–186.

——, "The DQDB Protocol and its Performance Under Overload Traffic Conditions," *Computer Networks and ISDN Systems*, vol. 20, no. 1–5, Dec. 1990, pp. 261–270.

M. Zukerman, L. J. Yao, and P. G. Potter, "DQDB Performance Under Sustained Overload with Bandwidth Balancing and Multiple Requests Outstanding," *Computer Communications*, vol. 16, no. 1, Jan. 1993, pp. 5–12.

D. ISDN AND BISDN

H. Aldermeshian, "ISDN Standards Evolution," *AT & T Technical Journal*, vol. 65, no. 1, 1986, pp. 19–25.

C. P. Anderson, "ISDN Market Opportunity," *IEEE Communications Magazine*, vol. 25, no. 12, Dec. 1987, p. 55.

J. Anderson, "International Standards for the Broadband ISDN User-Network Interface," *International Journal of Digital and Analog Communication Systems*, vol. 4, no. 2, 1991, pp. 143–150.

Anonymous, "ISDN—A World of Services," *Electrical Communication*, vol. 65, no. 1, 1991, pp. 22–26.

K. Asatani, "Lightwave Subscriber Loop Systems Toward Broadband ISDN," *Journal of Lightwave Technology*, vol. 7, no. 11, Nov. 1989, pp. 1705–1714.

——, "CCITT Standardization of B-ISDN," *NTT Review*, vol. 3, no. 3, 1991, pp. 122–133.

R. Y. Awdeh, "Why Fast Packet Switching?" *IEEE Potentials*, April 1993, pp. 10–12.

R. A. Boulter, "Access to a Broadband ISDN," *British Telecom Technology Journal*, vol. 9, no. 2, 1991, pp. 20–25.

W. Byrne, G. W. R. Luderer, G. Clapp, B. L. Nelson, and H. J. Kafka, "Evolution of Metropolitan Area Networks to Broadband ISDN," *IEEE Communications Magazine*, Jan. 1991, pp. 69–82.

W. R. Byrne, A. Papanicolaou, and M. N. Ransom, "World-Wide Standardization of Broadband ISDN," *International Journal of Digital and Analog Cabled Systems*, vol. 1, 1988, pp. 181–192.

R. C. Campbell and S. J. Sobel, "AT&T Aggressively Moves ISDN Forward," *AT&T Technology*, vol. 6, no. 1, 1991, pp. 22–29.

D. L. Carney and E. M. Prell, "Planning for ISDN in the 5ESS Switch," *AT&T Technical Journal*, vol. 65, no.1, Jan./Feb., 1986, pp. 35–43.

F. D. Castel, G. Pays, and G. Brillet, "Terminals for the ISDN Era: From Speech to Image," *IEEE Communications Magazine*, vol. 25, no. 3, 1987, pp. 39–43.

P. Chen, "How to Make the Most of ISDN's New LAPD Protocol," *Data Communications*, vol. 16, Aug. 1987, pp. 153–162.

T. M. Chen and D. G. Messerschmitt, "Integrated Voice/Data Switching," *IEEE Communications Magazine*, vol. 26, no. 6, 1988, pp. 16–26.

T. Cox *et al.*, "SMDS: The Beginning of WAN Superhighways," *Data International Communications*, April 1991, pp. 105–110.

R. Dawes, "An Introduction to ISDN Concepts," *Elektron*, vol. 5, no. 7, July 1988, pp. 14–15.

A. Day, P. Kirton, and J. Park, "Broadband ISDN and Fast Packet Switching," *Telecommunication Journal of Australia*, vol. 39, no. 1, 1989, pp. 29–36.

M. De Prycker, "Evolution from ISDN to BISDN: A Logical Step Towards ATM," *Computer Communications*, vol. 12, no. 3, 1989, pp. 141–146.

——, *Asynchronous Transfer Mode: Solution for B-ISDN*. London: Ellis Horwood, Prentice-Hall, 1990.

——, "ATM Technology: A Backbone for High Speed Computer Networking," *Computer Networks and ISDN Systems*, vol. 25, no. 4–5, Nov. 1992, pp. 357–362.

M. Decina, "Progress Towards User Access Arrangements in Integrated Services Digital Networks," *IEEE Transactions on Communications*, vol. COM-30, no. 9, Sept. 1982, pp. 2117–2130.

R. G. DeWitt, "ISDN Symposia: A Historical Overview," *IEEE Communications Magazine*, vol. 28, no. 4, 1990, pp. 10–11.

C. Dhas, V. K. Konangi, and M. Sreetharan (eds.), *Broadband Switching: Architectures, Protocols, Design, and Analysis*. Los Alamitos, CA: IEEE Computer Society Press, 1991.

G. H. Domann, "B-ISDN," *Journal of Lightwave Technology*, vol. 6, no. 11, Nov. 1988, pp. 1720–1727.

C. J. Dougall, "Broadband Network Evolution in Telecom Australia," *IEEE Communications Magazine*, vol. 28, no. 4, 1990, pp. 52–54.

R. N. Dunbar, "Design Considerations for Broadband Coaxial Cable Systems," *IEEE Communications Magazine*, vol. 24, no. 6, 1986, pp. 24–37.

J. Duncanson and J. Chew, "The Ultimate Link?" *Byte*, July 1988, pp. 278–286.

D. L. Eigen, "Narrowband and Broadband ISDN CPE Directions," *IEEE Communications Magazine*, April 1990, vol. 28, no. 4, pp. 39–46.

W. E. Falconer and J. A. Hooke, "Telecommunications Services in the Next Decade," *Proceedings of the IEEE*, vol. 74, no. 9, Sept. 1986, pp. 1246–1261.

N. S. Favre and J. L. Johnson, "AT&T's 5ESS Switch makes ISDN work," *AT&T Technology*, vol. 4, no. 3, 1989, pp. 12–19.

J. Filipiak, "Shaping Interworking MANs into an Evolving B-ISDN," *Computer Networks and ISDN Systems*, vol. 20, 1990, pp. 343–349

M. Frame, "Broadband Services Needs," *IEEE Communications Magazine*, vol. 28, no. 4, 1990, pp. 59–62.

M. Gerla, T. Y. C. Tai, and G. Gallassi, "Internetting LAN's and MAN's to B-ISDN's for Connectionless Traffic Support," *IEEE Journal on Selected Areas in Communications*, vol. 11, no. 8, Oct. 1993, pp. 1145–1159.

W. S. Gifford, "ISDN Performance Tradeoffs," *IEEE Communications Magazine*, vol. 25, no. 12, Dec. 1987, pp. 25–29.

C. W. B. Goode, "Broadband Services and Applications," *Electrical Communication*, vol. 64, no. 2/3, 1990, pp. 124–131.

D. Gulick and C. Crowe, "Interface the ISDN to Your PC with a Voice/Data Board," *Electronic Design*, Dec. 10, 1987, pp. 85–88.

R. Handel, "Evolution of ISDN Towards Broadband ISDN," *IEEE Network*, vol. 3, no. 1, Jan. 1989, pp. 7–13. Also in B. G. Kim (ed.), *Current Advances in LANs, MANs, and ISDN*. Norwood, MA: Artech House, 1989, pp. 302–308.

R. Handel and M. N. Huber, *Integrated Broadband Networks*. Reading, MA: Addison-Wesley, 1991.

J. Hartl and R. Schott, "Next Stop: ISDN," *Telcom Report*, vol. 13, no. 1, 1990, pp. 24–26.

H. J. Helgert, *Integrated Service Digital Networks: Architecture, Protocols, Standards*. Reading, MA: Addison-Wesley, 1991.

M. L. Higdon, J. T. Page, and P. H. Stuntebeck, "AT & T Communications ISDN Architecture," *AT & T Technical Journal*, vol. 65, no.1, Jan./Feb., 1986, pp. 27–33.

D. T. Huang and C. F. Valenti, "Digital Subscriber Lines: Network Considerations for ISDN Basic Access Standard," *Proceedings of the IEEE*, vol. 79, no. 2, Feb. 1991, pp. 125–143.

F. C. Iffland, G. D. Norton, and J. M. Waxman, "ISDN Applications: Their Identification and Development," *IEEE Network Magazine*, Sept. 1989, pp. 6–11.

Y. Inoue and M. Kawarasaki, "Networking Toward B-ISDN," *NTT Review*, vol. 3, no. 3, 1991, pp. 34- -43.

H. Ishii, "ISDN User-Network Interface Management Protocol," *IEEE Network Magazine*, Sept. 1989, pp. 12–16.

P. Kahl, "ISDN Implementation Strategy of the *Deutsche Bundespost Telekom*," *IEEE Communications Magazine*, vol. 28, no. 4, 1990, pp. 47–51.

S. Kano, K, Kitami, and M. Kawarasaki, "ISDN Standardization," *Proceedings of the IEEE*, vol. 79, no. 2, Feb. 1991, pp. 118–124.

J. J. Kauza, "ISDN: A Customer's Service," *AT&T Technology*, vol. 4, no. 3, 1989, pp. 4–11.

A. J. Kennedy and D. C. C. Yen, "The Coming ISDN," *Information and Management*, vol. 17, no. 5, 1989, pp. 267–275.

A. Kestes, "Integrated Services Digital Network S-Bus Design," *Electronic Engineering*, vol. Oct. 1987, pp. 77–82.

L. Kleinrock, "ISDN—The Path to Broadband Networks," *Proceedings of the IEEE*, vol. 79, no. 2, Feb. 1991, pp. 112–117.

R. Kopeikin, "ISDN Professional Service," *Electrical Communication*, vol. 63, no. 4, 1989, pp. 366–373.

J. Lamont and M. H. Hui, "Some Experience with LAN Interconnection via Frame Relaying," *IEEE Network Magazine*, Sept. 1989, pp. 21–24, 36.

R. Liebscher, "Strategies for the Successful Introduction of ISDN," *Electrical Communication*, vol. 64, no. 1, 1990, pp. 4–14.

S. H. Leibson, "Integrated Service Digital Network," *EDN*, Nov. 12. 1987, pp. 118–128.

M. Leonard, "ISDN: Approaching the End of the Tunnel," *Electronic Design*, Jan. 25, 1990, pp. 45–50.

I. M. Leslie, D. R. McAuley, and D. L. Tennenhouse, "ATM Everywhere?" *IEEE Network*, Mar. 1993, pp. 40–46.

M. Littlewood, "Metropolitan Area Networks and Broadband ISDN: A Perspective," *Telecommunication Journal of Australia*, vol. 39, no. 2, 1989, pp. 37–44.

P. Marsden, "Interworking IEEE 802/FDDI LAN's via the ISDN Frame Relay Bearer Service," *Proceedings of IEEE*, vol. 79, no. 2, Feb. 1991, pp. 223–229.

K. Martersteck, "ISDN Delivers the 90s Technologies Today," *AT&T Technology*, vol. 5, no. 1, 1990, pp. 2–3.

B. McNinch, "ISDN: The Man-Machine Interface," *IEEE Communications Magazine*, vol. 25, no. 12, 1987, pp. 50–54.

S. E. Minzer, "Broadband ISDN and Asynchronous Transfer Mode (ATM)," *IEEE Communications Magazine*, vol. 27, Sept. 1989, pp. 17–24. Also in C. Dhas, V. K. Konangi, and M. Sreetharan (eds.), *Broadband Switching: Architectures, Protocols, Design, and Analysis*. Los Alamitos, CA: IEEE Computer Society Press, 1991, pp. 81–89.

J. F. Mollenauer, "Metropolitan Area Networks and ATM Technology," *International Journal of Digital and Analog Cabled Systems*, vol. 1, no. 4, Feb. 1988, pp. 225–228.

——, "Metropolitan Area Networks Update: The Global LAN is Getting Closer," *Data Communications International*, Dec. 1989, pp. 109–118.

D. Morgan, M. Lach, and R. Bushnell, "ISDN as an Enabler for Enterprise Integration," *IEEE Communications Magazine*, vol. 28, no. 4, 1990, pp. 23–27.

K. Murano, K. Murakami, E. Iwabuchi, T. Katsuki, and H. Ogasawara, "Technologies Toward Broadband ISDN," *IEEE Communications Magazine*, vol. 28, no. 4, 1990, pp. 66–70.

J. L. Neigh and L. A. Spindel, "The Role of ISDN in AT&T Information Systems Architecture," *AT&T Technical Journal*, vol. 65, no. 1, Jan./Feb., 1985, pp. 45–55.

Y. Nishino and H. Oikawa, "An ISDN Basic Feature Telephone Set," *NTT Review*, vol. 3, no. 2, March 1991, pp. 89–97.

S. Ohtomo and S. Ishikawa, "Overview of ISDN Product and Service Development Programs at NTT," *NTT Review*, vol. 1, no. 2, July 1989, pp. 53–60.

S. H. Pandhi, "The Universal Data Connection," *IEEE Spectrum*, July 1987, pp. 31–37.

J. F. Patterson and C. Egido, "Three Keys to the Broadband Future: A View of Applications," *IEEE Network Magazine*, March 1990, pp. 41–47.

M. Rahnema, "Frame Relaying and the Fast Packet Switching Concepts and Issues," *IEEE Network Magazine*, July 1991, pp. 18–23.

D. Richards and E. Vogt, "The Value of ISDN for Banking Applications," *IEEE Communications Magazine*, vol. 28, no. 4, 1990, pp. 32–33.

M. M. Roberts, "ISDN in University Networks," *IEEE Communications Magazine*, vol. 25, no. 12, 1987, pp. 36–39.

G. Robin and S. R. Treves, "An Introduction to Integrated Services Digital Networks," *Electrical Communication*, vol. 56, no. 1, 1981, pp. 4–16.

R. T. Roca, "ISDN Architecture," *AT & T Technical Journal*, vol. 65, no. 1, 1986, pp. 5–17.

E. Y. Rocher, "Information Outlet, ULAN versus ISDN," *IEEE Communications Magazine*, vol. 25, no. 4, April 1987, pp. 18–32.

R. Roy, "ISDN Applications at Tenneco Gas," *IEEE Communications Magazine*, vol. 28, no. 4, April 1990, pp. 28–30.

M. N. O. Sadiku, "Integrated Services Digital Network," in G. McClein (ed.), *Handbook of Networking and Connectivity*, in press.

S. Sakata, "B-ISDN Multimedia Workstation Architecture," *IEEE Communications Magazine,* Aug. 1993, pp. 64–67.

F. Seveque and T. Wichers, "In-House ISDN Applications," *Electrical Communication*, vol. 63, no. 1, 1989, pp. 17–24.

J. Shandle, "ISDN: This Time It's For Real," *Electronics*, vol. 64, no. 5, May 1991, pp. 65–68.

W. Stallings, *ISDN: An Introduction.* New York: St. Martin's, 1989.

——, *ISDN and Broadband.* New York: Macmillan, 1992.

——, (ed.), *Advances in ISDN and Broadband ISDN.* Los Alamitos, CA: IEEE Computer Society Press, 1992.

P. D. Stigall and C. Blagioli, "SONET Utilization from FDDI Sources," *Computers and Electrical Engineering,* vol. 18, no. 5, 1992, pp. 373 388.

R. W. Stephenson and S. A. McGaw, "Southwestern Bell Telephone's ISDN Experience," *IEEE Network Magazine*, Sept. 1989, pp. 25–36.

M. Sterba, "ISDN in European Research Networking," *Computer Networks and ISDN Systems*, vol. 25, no. 4–5, Nov. 1992, pp. 400–404.

L. L. Stine, "Why Are ISDN Standards Important?" *IEEE Communications Magazine*, vol. 26, no. 8, 1988, pp. 13–15.

G. Stix, "Telecommunications," *IEEE Spectrum*, vol. 27, no. 6, 1990, pp. 25–26.

C. Strathmeyer, "Voice/Data Integration: An Applications Perspective," *IEEE Communications Magazine*, vol. 25, no. 12, 1987, pp. 30–35.

E. E. Summer, "ISDN: The Telephone of Tomorrow," *Radio Electronics*, Oct. 1988, pp. 41–50.

S. L. Sutherland and J. Burgin, "B-ISDN Interworking," *IEEE Communications Magazine,* Aug. 1993, pp. 60–63.

S. E. Swedan, D. G. Smith, and J. L. Smith, "Performance Advantage of Introducing an Abort Function into the DASS ISDN Protocol," *Journal of the Institution of Electronics and Radio Engineers,* vol. 56, no. 4, April 1986, pp. 151–158.

E. D. Sykas, K. M. Vlakos, and M. J. Hillyard, "Overview of ATM Networks: Functions and Procedures," *Computer Communications,* vol. 14, no. 10, 1991, pp. 615–626.

A. Takase, J. Yanagi, and Y. Miyamori, "Broadband Subscriber Loop Systems," *Hitachi Review,* vol. 40, no. 3, 1991, pp. 199–204.

M. W. Thomas, "ISDN: Some Current Standard Difficulties," *Telecommunication Magazine,* June 1991. Also in W. Stallings (ed.), *Advances in ISDN and Broadband ISDN.* Los Alamitos, CA: IEEE Computer Society Press, 1992, pp. 39–44.

S. Timms, "Broadband Communications: the Commercial Impact," *IEEE Network Magazine,* July 1989, pp. 10–15. Also in W. Stallings (ed.), *Advances in ISDN and Broadband ISDN.* Los Alamitos, CA: IEEE Computer Society Press, 1992, pp. 157–163.

I. Toda, "Migration to Broadband ISDN," *IEEE Communications Magazine,* vol. 28, no. 4, 1990, pp. 55–58.

J. S. Turner, "Design of an Integrated Services Packet Network," *IEEE Journal on Selected Areas in Communications,* vol. 4, no. 8, Nov. 1986, pp. 1373–1380.

I. S. Venieris, J. D. Angelopoulos, and G. I. Stassinopoulos, "Efficient Use of Protocol Stacks for LAN/MAN– ATM Interworking," *IEEE Journal on Selected Areas in Communications,* vol. 11, no. 8, Oct. 1993, pp. 1160- -1171.

K. W. Waber, "Considerations on Customer Access to the ISDN," *IEEE Transactions on Communications,* vol. COM-30, no. 9, Sept. 1992, pp. 2131–2136.

S. A. Wakid and K. Roberts, "Application Profile for ISDN," *Proceedings of the IEEE,* vol. 79, no. 2, Feb. 1991, pp. 199–204.

W. W. Wu and Adam Livne, "ISDN: A Snapshot," *Proceedings of the IEEE,* vol. 79, no. 2, Feb. 1991, pp. 103–111.

G. L. Zielinski, "ISDN Technology–Serving Industry Today," *AT&T Technology,* vol. 5, no. 1, 1990, pp. 4–11.

INDEX